Camaro

Anthony Young

MBI Publishing Company

First published in 2000 by MBI Publishing Company,
729 Prospect Avenue, PO Box 1, Osceola, WI 54020-0001USA

MBI Publishing Company books are also available at discounts in bulk quantity for industrial or sales-promotional use. For details write to Special Sales Manager at Motorbooks International Wholesalers & Distributors, 729 Prospect Avenue, PO Box 1, Osceola WI, 54020 USA.

Library of Congress Cataloging-in-Publication Data

Young, Anthony.
        Camaro / Anthony Young.
              p.   cm.
        Includes index.
        ISBN 0-7603-0783-0 (hc : alk. paper)
        1. Camaro automobile—History. I. Title.
TL215.C33Y68   2000
629.222'2--dc21   00-041837

On the front cover: More than 30 years separates two of the most powerful and fastest Camaros ever built. In the foreground is the 1969 Yenko/SC, powered by a 427-ci big-block V-8. In the background is the reigning heir to Camaro performance: the 2000 SS with a top speed capability of 160 miles per hour. *David Newhardt*

On the frontis piece: This Camaro carries the badge of modern muscle—SS. With a 305-horsepower 350-ci V-8, the 2000 Camaro SS ushered high performance into the twenty-first century. *David Newhardt*

On the title page: In its third year of production, the 1969 Z28 resided at the top of the small-block V-8 musclecar heap. Mark Donohue, driving a Roger Penske-prepared Z28, won the 1969 Trans-Am championship. The Z28 had some of the most handsome lines of any musclecar and could unleash blistering performance above 3,000 rpm. It remains the most famous performance name in the minds of "bowtie" lovers around the world. *Mike Mueller*

On the back cover: Top: One of the most attractive muscle cars to ever roll out of Detroit was the 1970 Z28. The wind-cheating profile of the second generation was launched in 1970, and that year's Z28 featured a 360-horsepower 350-ci LT1 solid lifter V-8. *Mike Mueller* **Bottom:** When the IROC-Z was introduced in 1985, it was offered as a separate option from the Z28. By 1988 it became a distinct model in the Camaro line, and the Z28 moniker was dropped. The IROC-Z featured aluminum wheels, special suspension parts, Delco/Bilstein shocks and front frame reinforcement. This is a 1990 IROC-Z finished in black. *David Newhardt*

Edited by Paul Johnson
Cover Design by Dan Perry
Text layout by Bruce Leckie
Designed by Tom Heffron

Printed in Hong Kong

CONTENTS

The Camaro SS became synonymous with stylish, affordable performance in the late 1960s. It garnered Best Sporty Car honors in Car & Driver's *1969 Readers' Choice Poll.*

Several key individuals made the task of writing about one of Chevrolet's most successful cars easier. Over the years, Jack Underwood of *GM Powertrain* has been generous in supplying me with information and photos on a wide range of Chevrolet cars and engines. For this book on the Camaro, he outdid himself. He told me only that he had collected a bunch of stuff on the Camaro since the late 1960s and he would be happy to send it to me. "You have a 'care package' on the way," Jack telephoned me one day. The "care package" I picked up at UPS weighed nearly 30 pounds! It was a treasure trove of magazines, MVMA specifications, photographs, slides, advertisements, and brochures. Thanks a million, Jack.

I would like to thank Joyce Deck of Chevrolet Communications for supplying the transparencies and information on the 2000 Camaro. Jody

Messinger of SLP Engineering also supplied me with information and transparencies of the SS.

The majority of color photographs in this book were the product of two of the finest automotive photographers today. Mike Mueller has supplied his excellent photography for several of my books, and we collaborated on *Chevrolet's Hot Ones: 1955, 1956, 1957* published by Motorbooks International in 1995. David Newhardt scoured southern California, photographing beautifully preserved examples of Camaros to include in this book. Bob Tronolone, a veteran race car photographer for four decades, supplied numerous shots for chapter 10.

There are cult movie enthusiasts and there are cult Camaro enthusiasts. One such Camaro group has formed around the 1LE-equipped IROC-Zs and Z28. This option was also available on GM's other F-body, the Firebird. The 1LE Owners Association came to me via the Internet with loads of information in the form of scanned and photocopied articles that are all but impossible to find today. Those individuals are Ryan Sebastian, president of the 1LE Owners Association (www.1LEOA.net); Joe Reece, who mailed me copies of all the 1LE articles in his possession; and Duncan Morrow, who sent me scanned articles I had not found anywhere else.

Bob Ashton of Auto Know in Utica, Michigan, generously loaned me the many Camaro advertisements you see in this book. Bob has helped me with two previous book projects, and his help with these Camaro ads added immeasurably to the book.

Jerry Ormand of Lago Vista, Texas, not only permitted me the pleasure of photographing his stunning 1999 SS, he also allowed me to drive it as it was meant to be driven, something he has allowed no one else to do. Thanks, Jerry. I came across Ken Spinks' 1991 Z28 convertible one day at work and was able to get his gleaming white steed down on celluloid.

Michael Hall of the Camaro and Firebird Car Club of Dallas/Fort Worth, Texas, came through at the last moment and put me in touch with owners of cars

I needed for the book. They include Mark Bellissimo and his 1984 Z28, Adam Billing and his 1987 Z28, Greg Blakely and his 1991 1LE IROC-Z, and Bob Routt and his restored 1973 Z28.

I would like to thank the editors for permission to quote from *"CAMARO: From Challenger to Champion,"* written by Gary Witzenberg.

The inspiration for this book came through a phone call from Paul Johnson, acquisition editor at Motorbooks. Paul helped me to structure the chapters in a logical form, carefully edited the manuscript, and kept a watchful eye over its layout in production.

This book is dedicated to hundreds of thousands of people who have a special place in their heart for the Camaro they used to own, proudly own today, and the Camaro they hope to own in the future.
—*Anthony Young*

In the late 1990s, the Camaro SS returned to an eager niche market. Its level of acceleration, handling and top speed of 160 miles per hour qualified it as one of the best performance cars in the world.

Many cars that molded aspirations and fulfilled dreams have entered into the American conscience. At the very top of this list is the Chevrolet Camaro. It was created as a stylish car for Everyman—and Everywoman. The Camaro had universal appeal. Although conceived during the musclecar era of the 1960s, when 300-plus horsepower was the domain of men, Chevrolet knew the Camaro would—and should—appeal to women as well. The Camaro that was introduced in the fall of 1966 was marketed to mold the aspirations and fulfill the dreams of both men and women.

The Camaro did not break new ground in creating an automotive genre. That honor belongs to the Ford Mustang. General Motors (GM) executives sat stunned as they watched enthusiasm for and sales of the Mustang take off. By the end of the 1965 model year, over half a million Mustangs were sold. GM had been caught flat-footed. How had this happened?

The postwar market of the early 1950s was very closely examined by GM executives, who set about building cars for young and prospering, yet frugal, Americans. Chevrolet Division was really on the ball here. The company introduced the Corvette in 1953, and the completely new Chevrolet in 1955; both these cars were clear market successes. The Corvair was introduced in 1960 for the economy car segment, and the Nova compact was unveiled for the same market in 1964.

Despite its innovations, GM had overlooked an emerging market niche—one that was hard to detect because it had not yet been defined. When Ford introduced the Mustang in mid-1964, GM quickly learned what that niche was. There were youthful buyers out there who wanted a sporty, stylish car with more seating and trunk capacity than the Corvette and more performance than the Nova could provide. And many first-time buyers were not so sure of that rear-engine Corvair.

Chevrolet designed the Z28 to compete in SCCA Trans-Am competition. Z28 was simply an RPO code, but it went on to become one of the most recognizable and famous names in Chevrolet history.
Mike Mueller

Chevrolet has always played off the similarities between the Camaro and the Corvette. The Corvette has always held a slight performance edge, but has always been more expensive. This ad appeared in 1971.

The GM board meetings were awash in Mustang brochures, road tests, magazine ads, and anything having to do with the Mustang. GM quickly initiated market studies that identified the emerging niche market. This new generation of youthful buyers were the sons and daughters of the men who had come home from fighting World War II. Watching the undeniable and unforeseen success of the Mustang, GM decided to fight for some of these buyers.

It was not long after the Mustang made its big splash—sometime late in 1964—that a decision was handed down from the GM board of directors. Chevrolet—the maker of America's only sports car—would build a car to compete with the Mustang. Chevrolet had no idea then the Camaro would go on to survive fierce competition from other quarters, rising insurance premiums and ever-tightening emission controls, economic recessions and several near-death experiences, and go on to become one of the more enduring names in automotive history. And for more than 30 years, the Camaro has been more than a match for the Mustang.

The Camaro rode the performance crest until it crashed in the early 1970s. When Chrysler ceased production of the Plymouth Barracuda and Dodge Challenger in 1974, Chevrolet kept the faith. The Camaro remained in production through the dark days of the 1970s, the era of catalytic converters and 5-mile per hour bumpers. Sales of the Camaro and the Z28—the most famous option code car in the world—continued to rise in the late 1970s to the mid-1980s. In 1984, over 100,000 Z28s were sold. Yet recession and a stock market collapse in the late 1980s took their toll on Camaro sales. The aging third-generation Camaro body contributed to declining sales in the early 1980s.

Rumors circulated predicting the demise of the Camaro. And just when many enthusiasts thought the Camaro would drive into the sunset, Chevrolet unveiled the strikingly sleek new Camaro in 1993—an aesthetic triumph. Performance was also on the rise again, with the return of the 350-ci V-8 in 1987, superseded by a new LT1 V-8 in 1993. The Camaro SS also returned in 1996 with even more performance, returning luster to the famous SS moniker.

The new millennium will see where the Camaro will go from here. It remains one of the most successful and memorable cars ever built by Chevrolet.

The fourth-generation Camaro was introduced in 1993. The optional tinted removable roof panels, or T-tops, gave the Camaro the best of both worlds: rigid coupe body with wind-in-the-hair excitement.

CHAPTER 1

CHEVY'S NEW MUSTANG CHALLENGER

1967 – 1969

The genesis of the Camaro may be traced back to 1964, and another manufacturer. On April 17 of that year, Ford introduced its new Mustang in dealer showrooms all across America. Unlike the abortive Edsel just a few years before, Ford had really done its homework on this car. From engineering to marketing, Ford was determined the new Mustang would succeed. And successful it was: 22,000 Mustangs were sold *on the very first day!* By the end of the year, Ford had moved over 263,000 of the model.

The public's excitement over the Mustang was unsettling to executives at General Motors. Nothing in any of its divisions was like the Mustang, and that was the problem. Some executives at GM argued the Mustang was not remarkable in any specific way, saying it was really style over substance. Yet none of these arguments mattered; the Mustang was selling like crazy. GM had been left in the starting gate with no horse of its own.

The first-generation Camaro remains handsome to this day, thanks to the aesthetic skill with which it was designed. Nose stripes, blackout grill, rear facia, and SS badging set the SS apart. Mike Mueller

The Camaro had gone through countless design studies, renderings, and clay models before finally settling on this one. This 1968 SS396 still turns heads today.
Mike Mueller

Chevrolet Gets a Reality Check

During a 1964 orientation meeting for summer interns working at General Motors, Vice President of Design Bill Mitchell, fielded questions from the young and enthusiastic group of students. He was asked when GM would have a car like the Mustang. Stoically, Mitchell responded, "We already have. It's called the Corvair."

Mitchell was putting on a brave face. Even he knew the Corvair was not a true competitor to the Mustang; it was a completely different car. On the other hand, Mitchell and other executives at GM felt the redesigned 1965 Corvair, especially with its optional supercharged flat-six engine, would give the Mustang a good run. Still, there were skeptics in the ranks at GM. Mitchell himself was pushing for a Corvair Super Spyder concept car. But General Manager Semon Knudsen (Bunkie) was hedging his bets. In the Chevrolet styling studios, he had his designers looking

at other sporty answers to Ford's surprisingly successful Mustang.

Some executives at GM were unaware of the Mustang's sales success. At one meeting at the GM building in downtown Detroit in the summer of 1964, they learned the stunning truth. In the four months since its introduction, the Mustang had sold over 100,000 units. It had become the fastest-selling new car in the entire history of the automobile. Skeptics turned realists almost immediately, and plans were launched to go head-to-head with Ford's pony car.

Knudsen was given corporate approval in August 1964 to immediately begin work on the new car. This was to be a crash program, and the car had to be introduced in the fall of 1966—only two years away. Chevrolet designers and engineers had an advantage, however. They had the Mustang as a gauge, and the goals were to make Chevrolet's new car superior in performance, handling, and above all, styling. More than a few Mustangs were already at Chevrolet's engineering center, some of them in pieces as engineers pored over the car to learn what Ford had done—and not done. Other Mustangs were out at GM proving grounds as test engineers tried to find out the Mustang's strengths and weaknesses.

With such a compressed design engineering schedule, the car could not be designed completely from scratch, but had to take into account concurrent engineering features on existing programs and incorporate them into the new car. GM was beginning to employ computer technology in a significant way in new vehicle engineering, and would use this technology for the new car. GM's Fisher Body Division would play a crucial role in this respect during chassis and body engineering.

For many years, cars had been built using a separate body and chassis, or frame. With this new car, Chevrolet was going to use the relatively new concept of unibody construction. This entailed designing a combined chassis/body structure from the firewall back. To this was bolted a stub-frame, which would accept the engine and all front suspension components. Chevrolet engineers had planned the unibody approach for the redesigned Chevy II Nova, due in 1968. It was an outgrowth of their dissatisfaction with the first-generation Chevy II in terms of its ride and handling. The new chassis configuration would benefit both cars.

Chevrolet's new "X" car would use a conventional suspension layout—unequal length control arms with coil-over-shocks in the front, and a live rear axle with leaf springs and shock absorbers in the rear. The Chevrolet small-block V-8 was going to be among the engine options, but executives took the long view and decided to engineer the car to accept the big-block V-8 then in development. This would prove to be a very profitable decision.

The one thing prospective buyers would see first would be the car's styling. It had to be absolutely right from the beginning. The GM division that produced the stunning 1963 and 1964 Corvette Sting Ray was certainly up to the task of designing a handsome skin for the new car. Irv Rybicki was group chief designer over the Chevrolet styling studios at the time. In charge of Studio No. 2 was Henry Haga, who would be responsible for the car's design. Haga, like Knudsen, sensed the Mustang might be "felt" at GM, and had his studio working on a Mustang-beater during the summer of 1964. Renderings and clay models were conspicuously present then, even before GM management gave Chevrolet approval to proceed.

Haga welcomed the opportunity to develop a four-place, two-door sporty car. Manufacturers made very little use of computers in the styling of cars in the early 1960s (though they did use them for engineering). Almost all body design was accomplished using renderings and clay models, both scale and full size. The limitations placed on engineering by the tight time constraints had virtually no effect on styling, allowing Haga's studio to start with a clean sheet of paper.

Exterior design of the car moved forward quickly. By the fall of 1964, full-size renderings depicting several different concepts had been completed. Some had a fastback configuration while others had a more conventional coupe roofline. From these early renderings evolved the scale and full-size clay mock-ups, an important phase that allowed the styling team to walk around the mock-up and subjectively evaluate and improve the design. The car's interior was also important, and was entrusted to George Angersbach. It was no easy task. To make sure he kept the theme of the car always in his mind, he actually bolted a four-speed shifter to his office chair.

The Camaro Evolves

Over the next year, the styling of the car evolved to nearly its final form. When the refined full-size clay buck was juxtaposed with a 1965 Mustang that December, Ford's pony car looked positively dowdy. The lines of the new Chevrolet were sweeping, clean and handsome. The Mustang looked as if it had already aged 10 years. Chevrolet Studio No. 2 was definitely on the right track.

Test mules of the car, thoroughly camouflaged with deceptive sheet metal and even cardboard, were running around GM's proving grounds in late 1965. These mules were also driven around Detroit and would always elicit double takes. Cross-country trips were also conducted as shakedown cruises, which are always part of any car's development program. Several significant problems arose during this time in the Camaro's development.

One involved the first Super Sport mule car. A development engineer, attempting to impress some wide-eyed parking attendants, did a burnout while turning out of the parking lot. The car exhibited severe wheel hop, something the engineer never had experienced with a live rear axle car. This was eventually resolved by using staggered rear shocks.

Many first-generation Camaros are meticulously restored, and this is evident under the hood of this 1968 SS396. The L78 big-block V-8 gave the Camaro a commanding presence on the street. **Mike Mueller**

This clay study shows the Camaro nearing its final form. One-piece door-glass was proposed as shown here, but the 1967 models featured vent windows.

A more worrisome problem was the cowl shake displayed by the convertible prototype. When hitting a bump or pothole, the car would continue to rack, or twist, for several seconds until the cycle subsided. The engineers tried everything they could think of to eliminate this cowl shake. Some solutions were successful but were not feasible to manufacture. Chevrolet engineering worked right up to the point of production to reduce the convertible's cowl shake, but they were never able to eliminate it completely.

The Camaro body that evolved had been wind tunnel tested and the "Coke bottle" shape proved to be aerodynamically clean. Besides the exposed

headlight design on the base model, Chevrolet also designed a Rally Sport model with concealed headlights, which gave the car an even cleaner look. The electrically powered headlight covers pivoted away when the headlights were turned on.

With all long-lead tooling ordered and the assembly lines established at Norwood, Ohio, and Van Nuys, California, the promotion mill started to crank up in 1966. The official name for the car had not been established yet; the working name for the car was Panther. Chevrolet's public relations office began working overtime, supplying the enthusiast magazines, newspapers, and other outlets with information on the upcoming car. Selecting the name for the car proved to be one of the most arduous steps in the whole vehicle program. It was a process that went on for months. Chevrolet employees were polled for suggested names, and they offered nearly 5,000 for consideration.

Chevrolet's merchandising manager, Bob Lund, was practically desperate to come up with a name because that, too, had to be tooled up. After considering every animal, mineral, vegetable, and celestial body, Lund felt the car should have a common first letter with Chevrolet's other models: Chevy II, Corvair, Chevelle, and Corvette. That narrowed things down a bit. One day, Lund and Ed Rollet, vice president of the GM Car and Truck Group, were going through a French-English and a foreign language dictionary. Suddenly, there it was: Camaro. Of the several definitions of this Spanish word, the one for "friend" did the trick. The more they spoke "Camaro," the more they both liked it. The search was over.

Chevrolet did not want to reveal too much about the car before its time, so many of the enthusiast magazines engaged in rampant speculation, complete with inaccurate illustrations and the Panther name. Some editors were downright cynical. The editors at *Car Life* complained the loudest:

"It probably should be called the Reluctant Dragon. It has been reluctant to arrive, its creators seem reluctant to build it, and the parent division is reluctant to admit its own two-year delay in recognizing this spectacular segment of the automotive market."

Finally, to put all rumors and false predictions to rest, Chevrolet's new general manager, Pete Estes, held a countrywide press conference—perhaps the largest "conference call" ever held, on June 29, 1966. Automotive editors collected in 14 U.S. cities around the country with Estes based in Detroit. Each press conference location had microphones and speakers, so everything discussed could be heard around the country. In his opening comments, Estes revealed the car's name and said, "The Camaro is aimed at the fast-growing personal sports-type market that was pioneered by Chevrolet's Corvette in 1953 and further

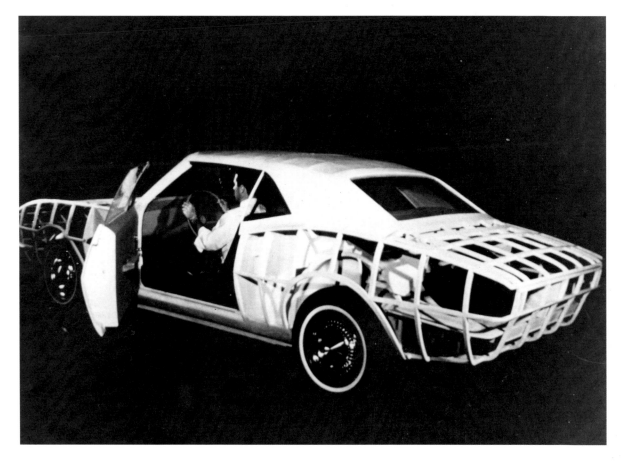

GM typically constructed a wood frame buck with all new car designs to check human factors. The fabric-over-frame construction inadvertently hinted that designers were concurrently working on a convertible.

indoor press conference room, the new Camaro was deliberately kept behind closed curtains while Estes explained to the press the market the car would appeal to—and it was a broad market. Estes said Chevrolet was capable of building over a quarter of a million Camaros a year, which took the wind out of a few of those present.

After making his presentation, he stepped back, the curtains parted, and the press for the first time saw the new Camaro. The car was an SS 350 convertible. As it slowly rotated on its turntable, Estes continued with his presentation. It was automotive razzmatazz at its best, and really got the press worked up. Later, the writers were permitted to get behind the wheel of all the 1967 Chevrolets, but everyone wanted to drive the new Camaro. It had a new 350-ci V-8, engineered specifically for the Camaro SS 350.

The L48 High-Performance 350 V-8

In 1965, when Chevrolet looked at the possibility of enlarging the small-block, Don McPherson was assistant chief engineer of passenger cars. Ed Cole had been the general manager of Chevrolet during development of the small-block but was promoted to group vice president in 1962. Bunkie Knudsen had become general manager, but Cole—always the engineer—kept a firm hand on the tiller at Chevrolet.

"Cole came along one day," McPherson remembers, "and got ahold of me and said, 'I want to go to 350 cubic inches and I want it all in bore.' It took me a month and a half to collar him and show him a layout proving it was pretty tough to have the pistons overlap one another. I said, 'Where do you want the flat spots on the rings?' He didn't like the sarcasm, but I said, 'We're just going to have to leave the 4.00-inch bore and stroke it' and that's what we did."

The task of designing the 350-ci V-8 fell to Dick Keinath and his V-8 engine group. It involved much more work than either the 283 or 327 had to undergo. It was not simply a matter of increasing the stroke from 3.25 inches to 3.48 inches.

"That was one engine where we had quite an argument going on whether we would be successful in getting that much displacement out of a small-block casting," Keinath recalls. " We agreed at the time that we were going to do it, but we were going to keep it as a passenger car version and try not to hotrod it, because we didn't think it would live. And,

Don McPherson was instrumental in the engineering of both the small-block and big-block V-8s at Chevrolet. He made the presentation to the GM board of directors that convinced the board to drop the 409-ci V-8 and build an all-new, better-breathing large-displacement V-8.

defined by the Corvair Monza in the 1960s." Estes cleverly sidestepped the issue of the Mustang and seized the high ground by tracing the Camaro's evolution back to the Corvette. The Camaro, however, would appeal to a new and different market.

On September 12, 1966, the Camaro was introduced to an expectant automotive press at the GM Proving Grounds. Estes deliberately saved the best for last, first going through each existing model and the new improvements and options for 1967, from the modest Chevy II to the exciting Corvette. In a large

of course, the argument always was, 'Once you get it out there, we're going to end up hot-rodding it because we always do.' No matter what, management assured me that they would avoid giving me a lot of problems, in performance and durability. We engineers down on the firing line felt that we were going to have to make it live regardless, so we just kept working hard on it.

"We raised the lower portion of the bore," says Keinath, "and made sure that there was enough room to swing the crankshaft in the panrail area, because we needed to get a better connecting rod in there. With a high stroke, we were throwing the piston off pretty fast and we needed to get a little more material into the connecting rod, which increased rotating and reciprocating weight. That meant we had to put bigger counterweights on the crankshaft, which meant we had to make sure there was room to swing the bigger counterweights, which in essence reduced the frequency of the crankshaft and made it more vulnerable to torsional breakage."

In an effort to alleviate these anticipated problems, the crankshaft journal diameters were increased for the first time since the small-block was introduced. Main journal diameter was increased to 2.45 inches and rod journal diameter was increased to 2.10 inches. The 350 crankshaft was cast nodular iron. It was considered perfectly adequate for use in anticipated passenger cars, but Keinath's worst fears were realized when he learned a high-performance version of the 350 would make its debut in none other than the Camaro SS 350. Sure enough, overzealous SS 350 drivers managed to wreak havoc with their engines, requiring warranty work. Under the repeated shock of clutch-dropping from redline, some engines suffered broken crankshaft noses, where the torsional damper would fall off and the Number One crankshaft arm would break. This was later solved in production by press-fitting the torsional damper and putting a drawbolt in the nose of the crankshaft. This preloaded the fillet where the nose turned down to the Number One main journal and reduced cyclic stress. The Number One arm cross-section was also beefed up. In the SS 350 Camaro, the L48 with 10.5 compression ratio and single Rochester four-barrel was rated at 295 horsepower at 4,800 rpm with 380 ft-lb of torque at 3,200 rpm. This engine was initially offered only in the Camaro SS.

The Press Responds

As it did for the Mustang, coverage of the Camaro by the automotive press would prove crucial. Hundreds of thousands of enthusiasts and curious prospective buyers eagerly snapped up *Car & Driver, Road & Track, Motor Trend, Hot Rod, Car Life,* and other magazines to learn everything they could about Chevrolet's new competitor to the Mustang. Among the first to get their hands on a test Camaro were the editors of *Car & Driver.* They didn't waste time with the standard Camaro model, but went right to the top of the performance heap by testing an SS 350. They

Chevrolet General Manager Semon Knudsen was the driving force behind the highly secretive Mk II 427-ci racing engine in the early 1960s. This led to the development of the production Mk IV big-block V-8 in 396- and 427-ci displacements.

Vince Piggins was in charge of Chevrolet Product Promotion— a nondescriptive title for engineer racing parts and vehicle development. He is recognized as the father of the Z28.

published their test results and reaction in the November 1967 issue.

The 295-horsepower V-8, four-speed manual transmission, and suspension settings made the Camaro SS 350 an enjoyable car for the editors to drive. But the bottom line was this car was neither superior nor inferior to the Mustang. It was entertaining, but it was no screamer. The car was virtually brand new and not broken in. It reached 60 miles per hour in 7.8 seconds and covered the quarter-mile in 16.1 seconds, tripping the timing lights doing 86.5 miles per hour. Summing up the car's performance, the editors wrote, "All told, Chevrolet's Camaro does not offer the extremes of performance that the Mustang does. GM's eggs are in a softer, more middle-of-the-road basket."

The editors at *Hot Rod* had a better car and a little more savvy in waking up the car's performance without getting inside the engine. They had racing great Bill Thomas—of Cheetah fame—give the car a super tune, performing basic hop-up tricks that could be done in anyone's garage. In stock trim the comparably equipped Camaro SS 350 covered the quar-

Camaro No. 3 was built at the Van Nuys, California, assembly plant. The Camaro Sport Coupe V-8 came standard with the 327-ci V-8. The only concessions the owner has made are the aftermarket wheels and tires.

ter-mile in 15.05 seconds doing 91 miles per hour. Thomas advanced the distributor curve, and added a new set of AC sparkplugs, improving the elapsed time to 14.95 doing 94 miles per hour.

At the debut of the Camaro in September, and during all subsequent road testing of the Camaro SS 350 by automotive journalists, the same question always arose: "Are you going to make the 396 big-block available in the Camaro SS?" The answer was "Yes, it would be offered later in the year." That was the news they wanted to hear. The 396 was the hot setup first in the Corvette, and then the Chevelle. The big-block in the Camaro would really make it a contender on the street.

The 396-ci Big-Block V-8

The modern big-block V-8 was much needed in the mid- and full-size Chevrolet line of cars, but in truth, this engine had its roots in racing. Don McPherson distinctly recalls how the new big-block V-8 engine project got started:

"Bunkie Knudsen didn't like the 409-ci engine. He asked us, 'Could we win Daytona with that

The third Camaro to roll off the assembly line in the fall of 1966 is still in the hands of the original owner. After returning from Vietnam and winning a high-stakes card game, the man took his winnings to the nearest Chevrolet dealer and bought this car off the lot. He has had many generous offers from people who want to buy his car, but he has refused them all.
David Newhardt

The body plate on the driver-side door jam of the 1967 Camaro was a simple one-line number. After some years the owner found out he owned the third Camaro built, and decided he would keep it.
David Newhardt

FRESH AIR INDUCTION DEVELOPMENT

The fresh air cowl induction was developed from tests conducted by Vince Piggins. In July 1962 Piggins sent driver Rex White and mechanic Louie Clemens to Daytona Speedway to conduct tests to find out why stock cars couldn't maintain a consistent top speed and why performance decreased slightly as the race wore on during a typical NASCAR event. Specifically, Piggins wanted to find out why a production Chevy 409 Biscayne was 1.5 to 2 miles per hour slower than a 380 Pontiac having 25 less horsepower. Piggins felt something else was going on under the hood.

"In conducting these tests, complete underhood environmental conditions were monitored in numerous locations giving us temperature and pressure readings in various locations, including the cowl plenum area that provides fresh air to the passenger compartment. Digesting and comparing the Chevrolet/Pontiac data, it was immediately eveident that conditions within the Pontiac engine compartment were both lower in temperature and slightly high pressure-wise in the immediate air cleaner area," Piggins said.

To simulate this condition in the Chevy, a hole was punched in the Biscayne's hood and a hood scoop was bolted over the hole near the carburetor intake. Rex White whipped the Chevy around Daytona's track and the instruments produced some startling numbers.

"This modification immediately increased the Chevy's top speed by 3 1/2 to 4 miles per hour per lap. Air pressure at the carburetor was raised to a level comparable to the Pontiac. However, the big change was the carburetor temperature being lowered from a previous 124 degrees Fahrenheit to 89 degrees Fahrenheit, or a 35 degree overall temperature reduction.

Camaro SS Sport Coupe with Super Scoop hood.

Camaro's New Super Scoop:
It's like frosting on the frosting.

Basic ingredients, Camaro SS, The Hugger: 300-hp 350 V8. Wide oval treads on 14 x 7 wheels. Beefed-up suspension. Power disc brakes. A floor-mounted 3-speed shifter.
Extra topping you can order: A new

Super Scoop hood that shoots cooler air to the carburetor for an added dash of dash.
The whole setup works off the accelerator. You step on the gas, *it* steps up top end power.

There you have it: Super Sport with Super Scoop.
Add you and stir.

Putting you first, keeps us first.

Chevy promoted the new Super Scoop in this ad. The Vince Piggins-designed air intake increased air pressure and lowered temparatures on the carburetor for a stronger fuel charge, thus more horsepower. Chevrolet

Obviously with underhood air intake, as the engine compartment temperature rose, the speed and power decreased," Piggins explained.

With these results in hand, Piggins requested a special hood manufactured for use on 1963 Chevrolets to qualify for NASCAR production rules. The cost of tooling was prohibitive and the request was turned down. Piggins was not daunted. In October 1963 Piggins conducted tests using fresh air drawn from the cowl area at the base of the windshield. A hole was made in the back of the 409's air cleaner and a fiberglass duct ran to a hole in the firewall which opened up into the plenum area. This way the engine would receive cool outside air that was also under pressure. The boost in performance matched that of the hood scoop approach. This form of fresh air induction was immediately put to use on Chevrolets competing the remainder of the 1962 NASCAR season.

It would be several years before fresh air induction would become available on performance Chevrolets for the street. It finally was offered on the 1967 Z28 as an option; code Z281. It included a modified air cleaner and ductwork to the firewall plenum area. The cost of the Z28 option with the fresh air underhood system was $479.25. It was offered again in 1968. In mid-1969, the first cowl induction hood was offered on the Camaro SS and Z28 under the RPO of ZL2 for a bargain price of $79.

Fresh air induction on the Camaro disappeared in 1970, but reappeared occasionally in the 1970s and 1980s. It returned again in the late 1990s on the SLP-developed, high-performance Camaro SS. Virtually all automobiles today benefit from fresh air induction via ductwork that runs from the grill area to the air cleaner.

engine?' and I told him no, we couldn't, because of the restrictions in it. He wanted an engine that would win Daytona. The assignment from Knudsen was to build an engine that would win Daytona and sell it to the corporation. That's how that engine got started."

As with the Chrysler 426 Hemi, which would come after it, racing was to be the crucible in which this new Chevrolet engine would be created, before it was offered in street tune in passenger cars. Chevrolet was adhering to the spirit, if not the letter, of the Automobile Manufacturers Association's (AMA) ban of direct involvement by car makers in racing.

Under the rule, the automakers could only supply engines used in production cars; they couldn't develop special racing engines. To undertake a racing engine program was really dicey—to say the least! How could the Chevrolet engineers do it under the watchful eyes of GM's board of directors?

To do this, Knudsen and McPherson had to build the case against the old 'W' engine, as it was referred to due to its valve configuration, and strongly promote the idea of a brand-new V-8. Pragmatic engineering and marketing reasons for building a new V-8 had to be presented in the context of passenger cars and trucks, if

The Camaro SS350 was a conservative approach to sporty performance. In 1967, buyers could choose between coupe and convertible. This SS came with the RS option, which featured concealed headlights.
Mike Mueller

The Camaro shared body structure, some sheet metal, and all glass area with the Pontiac Firebird. Despite this, the Camaro retained its unique look. The SS350 convertible was a great blend of top-down performance and style.
Mike Mueller

this engine was ever going to fly. The task of getting approval for the new engine fell to McPherson.

"I had the job of selling the corporation on the fact that Mr. Cole's engine—the 'W' engine from engineering staff—was no good and had to be replaced by the Mark [for Mark II, or second V-8 engine]," McPherson recalls. "I had to go before the engineering staff and the executive committee downtown, including the president and chairman of GM, at the GM building, and sell this thing. We pretty much stated the facts as to the problems with breathing on the W and

with surface-to-volume in the combustion chamber. The thing made engineering sense, and everybody bought it. It took about half an hour."

McPherson chose Dick Keinath to lead the small group designing the new engine. McPherson directed Keinath to design the new engine using more or less conventional valve configuration with the combustion chamber in the cylinder head, but McPherson emphasized the need for high rpm breathing ability. In order to utilize manufacturing line tooling and as many parts as possible, the 4.84-inch bore centers

and displacement of 409 cubic inches were retained. The most dramatic changes would occur to the cylinder head and intake manifold.

Flow studies centered around the intake and exhaust port design and the juxtaposition of the intake and exhaust valves. Unlike the small-block V-8 introduced in 1955, the intake and exhaust valves would not be parallel. Improved flow was achieved by tilting the intake valve toward the intake port, the exhaust valve toward the exhaust port, and then titling both valves away from each other by 8 degrees. This splayed valve configuration looked curious to say the least, and some clever individual coined the term "porcupine head" to describe it. Keinath and his small, clandestine team also did extensive work to reduce the mass of valvetrain components in order to increase top end horsepower. The design team also paid close attention to the exhaust side of things. The exhaust ports were designed virtually round, and the exhaust manifolds were essentially cast-iron headers; they worked beautifully.

"We procured many parts to reduce the mass of the valvetrain," says Keinath, "including shorter and lighter valve lifters and thinner valve spring caps.

The entire system was designed to run at high rpm in order to fully utilize the larger ports in the manifolds and cylinder heads for increased power."

The bottom end of the cylinder block, surprisingly, employed two-bolt main bearing caps. Chevrolet encountered few problems with the Z-11—the competition 409—and saw no reason to go to four-bolt mains with the Mk II.

Up top, the intake system employed a dual-plane 180-degree aluminum intake manifold and this, too, was subject to many hours of flow testing to produce the optimum level of performance near the engine's designed redline. The carburetor, naturally, was a Holley with 1 11/16-inch primary and secondary bores. The engine would incorporate the new cowl air intake system pioneered by Vince Piggins. This drew cooler, denser outside air from the base of the windshield, which boosted performance. This innovation would go on to set an industrywide trend in the late sixties.

Keinath and his team were well into the Mk II development program when NASCAR announced a change in displacement to 427 cubic inches. Keinath chose a longer stroke crank with correspondingly

Chevrolet snagged pace car duties for the 1967 Indianapolis 500. Chevrolet used this event to launch a Camaro Pacesetter sale on the six-cylinder model.

shorter connecting rods to achieve the displacement goal. These engines were called Mk IIS engines. The engines destined for Daytona for the 500 were meticulously assembled, tested at Chevrolet's Tech Center, crated, and shipped to the Florida track just days before the 100-mile qualifying races. Junior Johnson, Johnny Rutherford, Bubba Farr, C. G. Spencer, and Rex White would run their cars with this engine. No one but the drivers and team mechanics were permitted to look under the hoods of these Chevrolets. When Junior Johnson won the first qualifier and Rutherford the second with record average speeds, rumors began

flying all over Daytona about Chevrolet's new "Mystery Engine." The hoods stayed firmly closed.

Ford became suspicious and filed a complaint with NASCAR. The saga that evolved over the next week proved a cliffhanger for Chevrolet, which was almost disqualified from the race before it began. To "prove" the new engine was, in fact, in production, Chevrolet was forced to sell two of the engines to Ford! Only then was Chevrolet permitted to race the Daytona 500. Sadly, the cars did not hold up during the grueling race. The first five cars to get the checkered flag were Fords. McPherson and Knudsen were called to answer some probing questions by GM's board, but after the dust settled, the engine was approved for production in Chevrolet's cars and trucks.

Based on the development work of the Mk II, the Mk IV would be offered in 396-ci displacement beginning in 1965, and the 427 would appear in 1966. The 396 was offered in the Chevelle, Impala, and Corvette, and would be offered in the Camaro that was then under development. In November 1967, Camaro buyers had a choice of two 396 V-8s: the 325-horsepower hydraulic lifter L35, and the 375-horsepower mechanical lifter L78.

So—what was the price of Camaro big-block performance in its first year of production? Base list for the Camaro Sport Coupe V-8 with standard 327-ci V-8 was $2,572; the convertible was $2,809. The SS 350 option added $210.65. The 325-horsepower SS 396 option cost $263.30. The 375-horse 396 set you back $500.30. The four-speed manual transmissions were very popular options in the Camaro, and you had a choice of close or wide ratio. Either four-speed cost you $184.35. The superb Turbo HydraMatic transmission was $226.45. Tremendous torque made the 396 Camaro a good straight-line performer on the street, but the added weight caused handling to suffer.

Chevrolet had another high-performance version it planned to unveil in the last month of 1967: the Z28.

Z28: Contender for Trans-Am

In the mid-1960s, General Motors was laboring under a self-imposed racing ban to comply with the AMA ban on factory racing. Of course, there were no teeth behind this AMA edict. Ford chose to ignore the

ban and go racing. The company poured millions of dollars into its racing effort, looking for wins on practically all fronts. One of them was SCCA racing, using its Mustang, specifically Carroll Shelby's modified Mustangs. And win they did. In 1966, the SCCA instituted its Trans-Am series for two-door, four-passenger sedans, and the hot Mustangs were the hands-down winners.

In August 1966, Chevrolet's dynamic product promotion engineer, Vince Piggins, recommended to Pete Estes that a special performance package for the Camaro be offered after the Camaro was introduced. This would qualify the car for SCCA homologation and racing by independent teams. If the Trans-Am Camaros were successful on the track, it would certainly reflect positively on Camaro sales.

Estes authorized a prototype. If it looked good, he'd be willing to talk further. By October, Piggins had a prototype available he felt confident would convince Estes. The car had a high-performance 283. At the GM proving grounds, Piggins took the wheel for a test drive with Estes as passenger. Estes was impressed. Piggins suggested using the 327 with a 283 crankshaft, which would bring it to 302 cubic inches, just

The 327-ci small-block V-8 was a good balance of fuel economy and adequate performance in the Camaro. RPO L30 was rated at 275 horsepower (gross), and this option cost only $92.70. The L30 was the only optional small-block V-8 available in the Camaro as an engine only. The 302 and 350 were part of performance package options.

The 1965 Corvette introduced the 396-ci big-block V-8. The hydraulic lifter L35 and solid lifter L78 were added to the Camaro option list in November 1966. Performance development took place at Chevrolet's Engineering Center. Zora Arkus-Duntov is shown working with engineer Denny Davis in one of the Chevrolet dyno rooms at Chevrolet's Engineering Center in May 1966.

below the 5.0-liter limit set by the SCCA. Don McPherson was also at the Proving Grounds that day and was enthusiastic about the engine and vehicle program.

Bill Howell was one of Chevrolet's engine development engineers at the time, and he remembers the program well.

"At the time," Howell says, "in 1965 and 1966, we had the 283 and the 327. The 283 was the bread-and-butter engine and we no longer made the high-performance version of it in the 1965–66 era. We had the 327, which was the high-performance leader for the small-block. When the SCCA specked out their Trans-Am series, they did it at an engine size that Ford had, which was 302. We had an engine on either side of that but nothing that fit the category. It happened that the parts for the 283 and 327 were virtually interchangeable with regard to crankshaft size, main bearing size, and so on. You could put a 283 crankshaft in the 327 and take a quarter-inch of stroke away and it came up with 302 cubic inches. There were other types of racing where the racers

were already doing that, so it was not an unheard-of combination."

Dave Martens moved into Dick Keinath's V-8 engine group in 1965. This was one hot place for a Chevrolet engineer to be working in the mid-1960s. Now there was a new engine program under way in 1966—the high-performance 302.

"My first deep involvement in the engine was when it became 302 cubic inches for the Trans-Am series," recalls Martens. "I was project engineer and they gave me the responsibility for getting that engine to develop durability and power. At the same time, I was the design leader for that project with a man by the name of Jerry Thompson. Jerry was a laboratory engineer and he ran the dynamometer for power development. Roger Penske was a rising star at the time and he had an in with Chevrolet. He would come in and discuss things with the chief engineer on the project, Jim Musser."

The racing engine development was handled outside Chevrolet. The racing 302s were built by

Traco, the team of Travis and Coon in California, with the parts developed and supplied by Vince Piggins Product Promotion Group. Some of these Traco 302s were shipped to Piggins at the Chevrolet Engineering Center for evaluation. They certainly had an influence on the engineering development of the street 302. As developed for the Camaro, the street 302 was rated at 290 horsepower at 5,800 rpm with 290 ft-lb of torque at 4,200 rpm. The 302, having a 4 inch bore and 3-inch stroke, featured an 11.0:1 compression ratio; a specifically designed aluminum intake manifold fed by a Holley 800-cubic feet per minute (cfm) carburetor; a solid-lifter "30-30" camshaft designed by Denny Davis while in Zora

Arkus-Duntov's Corvette group and first used in the 1964–65 fuel-injected 327 Corvette; 2.02-inch intake and 1.60-inch exhaust valves; a forged crankshaft with a new Tufftriding surface treatment; forged pistons and premium connecting rods; an oil pan windage tray; a five-blade fan with viscous clutch; a special coil and distributor; and special dual exhaust designed for use with tube headers. A special air cleaner with plenum fresh air intake at the base of the windshield was to be offered as an option. The cars were shipped to dealers with cast-iron exhaust manifolds, and when the optional tube headers were ordered, they were placed in the Z28's trunk, and could be installed by the dealer upon delivery.

Nickey Chevrolet of Chicago was among the first dealers to offer specially modified Camaros fitted with 427-ci big-block power. Collectors prize these cars today.
Mike Mueller

"Stock-out-of-the-box 302s," says Howell, "under the gross horsepower test with the stock cam and exhaust manifold, were 340 to 350 horsepower. They underrated it somewhat for the street."

In its Trans-Am-inspired state of tune, the Z28 was not an ideal street machine. Dave Martens recalls it wasn't everyone's favorite car at Chevrolet.

"Don McPherson did not like the low-end torque—there wasn't any," Martens states. "It was a high-speed, high-performance engine. There wasn't any pulling power if you put it into fourth gear at 1,000 rpm. The original 302, with a mechanical camshaft, lasted only one year. It wasn't suitable for anyone wanting an automatic."

This is perhaps a valid complaint, but then, the Z28 was conceived for road racing and a street version had to be produced to satisfy the homologation rules. Besides, there were other engines available in the Camaro that were much more suitable for street

This decal appeared on the rear spoiler of the 1967 Nickey Camaro, and a discreet die-cast badge affixed to the front fenders above the special dual flag medallion announced the car's 427-ci V-8.

Nickey Chevrolet could install either the 400-horsepower L68 or the 435 horsepower L71 tripower 427-ci V-8s in its special Camaro. Chevrolet originally designed the two engines for the Corvette. Mike Mueller

use. In this light, the Z28 can be forgiven its road manners. The true character of the production Z28 came through in SCCA events, making the car a true, dual-purpose machine.

There was another aspect of the 1967 Z28 that had tremendous impact on the street: mystique. Just over 600 examples were built for that model year and seeing one on the road was rare. The Z28 Special Performance Package cost $358.10. However, if you also wanted the performance hood with plenum air intake and special air cleaner, the cost was $437.10. If you wanted the Z28 with the tube exhaust headers

shipped in the trunk, the option cost was $779.40. If you wanted "all of the above" it set you back $858.40.

Car & Driver tested a 1967 Z28 and achieved a 0–60 mile per hour time of 6.7 seconds, covering the quarter-mile in 14.9 seconds at 97 miles per hour. The editors heaped accolades upon the car: "The engine is obviously the Z28's strongest point. The 290-horsepower figure quoted for the Z28 engine seems ludicrously conservative; it feels at least as strong as the 327-ci, 350-horsepower hydraulic lifter engine offered in the Corvette.

All 1967 Camaros featured basically the same interior, with emphasis on warning lights instead of gauges. The large-diameter steering wheel was a necessity on Camaros without optional power steering.

Functional rear spoiler and hood and rear deck stripes distinguished the 1967 Z28 on the street, but no badges appeared anywhere to identify it as such. SCCA homologation rules required a minimum production run in order to compete in Trans-Am events.

"The 302 engine is without a doubt the most responsive American V-8 we've ever tested, although there is a trace of unevenness at low speeds because of the carburetor's unusually large venturi area. Once it begins to pull, however, it smoothes out and lunges forward like a 426 Hemi. The redline on the tach was at 5,500 rpm, which we and the engine cheerfully ignored. It revs quickly to 6,000 rpm, with no sign of getting tight, and we reluctantly shifted—in the interests of prudence."

All told, how well did the Camaro do in its first year of sales? According to Chevrolet, Camaro sales totaled 220,906. This was roughly half the sales of the Mustang that year, but a very good year nevertheless considering its come-from-behind situation. Chevrolet pulled off a marketing coup by landing the Camaro

pace car honors at the 1967 Indianapolis 500. Of course, few know about the wheeling and dealing that goes on behind the scenes for a manufacturer's car to be chosen to pace the field. Nevertheless, it gave Chevrolet untold prestige and priceless exposure to its brand-new pony car. Chevrolet did not offer a pace car replica for 1967. The division had enough new Camaro models to deal with. And it was working to get out the new Camaros for 1968.

Fine Tuning—1968 and 1969

On September 15, 1967, Chevrolet introduced the 1968 Camaro. There was no change to any sheet metal, only subtle but effective restyling to the front and rear end. Sharp eyes caught the fact that there

were no vent windows any longer; door glass was all one piece. Chevrolet had developed "Astro Ventilation" to permit a constant but undetectable flow of fresh air to the passenger compartment. Chevrolet had been working on the rear axle hop experienced by its high-performance models by adding multileaf rear spring rates and staggered rear shocks in an attempt to control it. The problem persisted but was less severe. Clearly, the aftermarket would have to be called on to improve the Camaro's "holeshot" behavior on the street and the strip.

Despite its small-block displacement, the Z28 managed to garner the majority of the enthusiast magazine coverage over the SS 350 and SS 396 Camaro. Piggins' team had continued development work on the production car and had new options available on the 1968 Z28. Chevrolet was not racing, of course, but Roger Penske and driver Mark Dono-hue sure were burning up the SCCA Trans-Am series with the Z28, and for 1968 they had a new weapon—a special dealer-installed option having two staggered 600-cubic feet per minute (cfm) Holley

The Z28 302-ci V-8 used newly designed heavy-duty parts, which were vital to its success in Trans-Am events across North America. These parts were also available through dealers.

Yenko Chevrolet of Pennsylvania became the best-known dealer offering Camaros with engines and equipment unavailable from Chevrolet. Yenko had a participating dealer network so buyers could order a Yenko without having to go to Pennsylvania.
Mike Mueller

carburetors atop a specially cast aluminum intake manifold with plenum fresh air intake, front and rear disc brakes, Koni shocks at all four corners, tube exhaust headers, heavy-duty valves springs, transistorized ignition, and heavy-duty clutch and flywheel. The dealer-installed racing package set you back $1,731.80. But then, this car was meant to go racing and beat the Mustangs while doing it.

This car was a screamer. While designed for such tracks as Laguna Seca, Limerock, and Riverside Race-

way, this Z28 did amazing things on the quarter-mile. It reached 60 miles per hour in 5.3 seconds, and covered the quarter-mile in 13.7 seconds doing 107.39 miles per hour through the Chrondecks.

The SS for 1968 could quickly be distinguished by its two nonfunctional but functional-looking hood intakes. Piggins had developed a new rear spoiler that appeared on the racing Camaros and worked quite well. It was available on street Camaros for 1968 as option D80 and cost a mere $32.65. Many

continued on page 36

The Hugger. Camaro SS Coupe with Rally Sport equipment.

What the younger generation's coming to.

The 1969 Camaro is closing the generation gap. Fast.

Some parents are even asking to borrow their kids' Camaros.

And some kids are actually letting them.

Camaro's secret is its Corvette accent. Standard bucket seats. V8's up to 325 horse-

See Olympic Gold Medalist Jean-Claude Killy, Sundays, CBS-TV. See your local TV listings.

power. And Camaro's the only American car besides Corvette that offers 4-wheel disc brakes.

Camaro's got a lot more going for it, too. Like this SS version that comes with a big V8, power disc brakes, beefed-up suspension, a special floor shift and wide oval tires. And with the Rally Sport package, you've got the only

sportster at its price with out-of-sight headlights.

But don't think for a minute that we won't sell you a Camaro if you're over thirty.

After all, it's not how young you are.

It's how old you aren't.

Putting you first, keeps us first.

CHEVROLET

The advertising budget for the Camaro permitted ads not only in enthusiast magazines but in larger format publications like LIFE and LOOK. This ad for the 1969 SS396 was directed to those in their 30s and 40s who wanted to count themselves as part of the younger generation.

FOR THOSE WANTING SOMETHING MORE...

With the introduction of the big-block 396 option in the Camaro, several Chevrolet dealers around the United States saw the possibility of offering customers even more performance—a level of performance Chevrolet and General Motors would not offer. While the 427-ci big-block V-8 was offered and sold in the Corvette and Impala, corporate edict prevented that option being offered in the Camaro. That edict stipulated no engine over 400-ci displacement would be installed in F-body Camaros or Firebirds. The 427 was only 30 ci or so larger in displacement. And its external dimensions were identical to the 396. What was the big deal?

For Chevrolet, perhaps it was a matter of the power-to-weight ratio. The Corvette had to be the fastest of all the Chevrolets, so only the Corvette got the tri-power L68 or L71, or full-race L88 427. The Impala could be ordered with the four-barrel 390 hp L36 427, but the top gun big-block in the 1967 Camaro was the 375 hp L78 396. Of course, this prompted the question, "Why not a SS427 Camaro?"

Several dealers around the country stepped up to the plate and decided to do just that. Today, these dealers have become legendary and the names of the Camaros they offered command some of the highest prices for musclecars of the late 1960s.

They included Nickey Chevrolet in Chicago, Illinois; Dana Chevrolet in Southgate, California; Yenko Chevrolet in Cannonburg, Pennsylvania; Berger Chevrolet in Grand Rapids, Michigan; and Baldwin Chevrolet in Long Island, New York. The dealers saw these supercars as a way to promote their names before thousands of prospective buyers by campaigning the cars in drag racing competition and receiving magazine coverage. While prospective buyers walking into the showroom may not sign for a big-block pavement pounder, the salesman might just steer them into something more practical.

These knowledgable dealers had professional high-performance mechanics who knew how to properly set up the 427 Camaros; it didn't stop with simply dropping in a 427 big-block V-8. Take for example the 427 offered by Nickey Chevrolet. The dealer hooked up with Bill Thomas Race Cars in Anaheim, California. Thomas had become famous for his incredi-

Send $1.00 for our all-new '69½ 396/427 Super-Chevy catalog

For most of the competition, the moment of truth against Baldwin Motion Phase III-427 Camaro was a losing moment. Rated at a conservative 425-horsepower, the Phase III was one of the fastest musclecars ever.

bly fast Cheetah race car. The Nickey/Bill Thomas 427 Camaro was offered in three different stages of performance and appearance. Beyond that, the buyer could tailor his Camaro to his specific needs or wants with a staggering array of speed equipment options. The list of standard equipment in each stage of the Nickey/Thomas 427 Camaro is too long to list here, but each car was engineered to get the power to the pavement and retain bulletproof reliability. Stage I cost $389.00, Stage II was $689.00, and Stage III—created to bring home the trophies—cost $1,089.00 above the MSRP for the SS396 Camaro.

Dana Chevrolet took much the same approach and drew upon the talents of Peyton Cramer, who had so successfully made Shelby-American a household name among Ford enthusiasts. The Dana 427 Camaro was also offered in three different stages of performance. To make this level of performance work, the suspension was beefed up, and wider wheels and fatter tires were stuffed into the wheelwells. Even with these improvements, it was easy to melt the tires in first gear with the 425 hp four-barrel 427 under the hood. It took supreme control to properly launch the car when accepting the stoplight challenge.

Motor Trend tested the Dana 427 Camaro for its July 1967 issue. The car had the optional Dana performance hood which helped to give it a distinctive and purposeful look. The car had so much power the editors had to launch the car in second gear; getting through the quarter-mile in 14.2 seconds doing 105 mph. Putting Goodyear racing slicks on the car dropped the elapsed time to 13.3 seconds at 107 mph. This car was fitted with tube headers for the high-performance exhaust system. Uncorking the headers to permit them to bypass the street exhaust system dropped elasped times even farther: 12.75 seconds doing 110 mph through the timing lights! The Dana 427 Camaro was among the fastest street machines anyone could buy.

Don Yenko was among the highest profiled Chevrolet dealers in the country and he worked to establish the sale of his Yenko Camaros through other dealers as well as his own. In other words, a customer could walk into a participating Chevrolet dealer and order a Yenko 427 Camaro. SS

Nickey was another performance shop that offered a wide range of high-performance parts and accessories for the Camaro. Each stage of performance was specifically designed for a certain performance level and budget.

350 Camaros were more plentiful, so Yenko used these to swap in the L72 and perform the other modifications needed. He built 54 examples of the Yenko 427 Camaro in 1967.

On Long Island, New York, Joel Rosen operated Motion Performance; essentially a speed shop and super tuning center. He hooked up with Baldwin Chevrolet, located a few blocks from his business, and convinced the dealer he could build high-performance Chevys that would put Baldwin Chevrolet on the map. The dealer took the gamble and the rest, as they say, is history. The Baldwin-Motion combination produced the Fantastic Five: SS-427 Camaro, SS-427 Chevy II, SS-427 Chevy Biscayne, SS-427 Corvette, and SS-427 Chevelle. The SS-427 Camaro, built by Rosen, featured the 425 hp L72 427; close ratio Muncie four-speed manual; choice of rear axle ratio, heavy-duty suspension, and radiator; Redline Wide Oval tires; engine dressup items; and distinctive emblems. The price was only $3,795. Over and above that, Rosen was happy to build your Camaro any way you wanted it, and Rosen could deliver the goods. Many Baldwin-Motion SS-427 Camaro owners took home trophies from their local drag strips.

The Berger 427 Camaros are perhaps the least-known among this group. Berger was the last to get into this niche market, and when a Berger 427 Camaro is spotted at a Chevy meet, it invariably is a 1969 model. In fact, Yenko was instrumental in convincing Chevrolet they were missing the boat on this opportunity. Chevrolet already had the apparatus in place to build very special vehicles—vehicles with options not on the Regular Production Option (RPO) list. This was achieved using the Central Office Production Order, or COPO. Vince Piggins set up the means of building 427 Camaros using the COPO procedure in 1969. There were two COPO Camaros you could order that year: COPO 9560, which was the ZL-1 aluminum 427 for full-race applications on the quarter-mile; and COPO 9561, which included the cast iron L72 427 with heavy-duty driveline, suspension, Positraction rear end, and cowl induction performance hood.

When the 454 replaced the 427 in 1970, most of the dealers upped the ante again, but it was Baldwin-Motion that was most visible in this effort. The big-block engine swaps came to an end when the Environmental Protection Agency cracked down on them. Today, these cars are among the most prized prosessions of automotive museums and car collectors today.

Chevrolet introduced the fresh air hood scoop on the Z28 in 1969; this functional hood was optional on other SS Camaros. The hood drew high-pressure air from the base of the windshield. Tests by Vince Piggins found a performance improvement over hot air drawn from the engine compartment. Mike Mueller

Camaro buyers that year opted for it. There were no changes to the performance specifications of the 350 or 396s available in the Camaro, but the engines were sporting new emissions control hardware and plumbing as stiffer EPA regulations kicked in for that year. *Car Life* tested the 1968 SS 396 Camaro. This car was equipped with a Turbo Hydra-Matic transmission. Trying to get all that power to the road without excessive wheelspin with the narrow bias-ply tires of the day was practically impossible. Performance figures were well below what the car

was capable of, no doubt also due to the newness of the car.

One of the first things serious street racers—uh—enthusiasts—did was put more rubber on those rims. This improved the car's handling and rear wheel traction. Also, more performance could be extracted from the big-block 396 using one of the three available four-speed manual transmissions. Over 47,000 Camaro buyers that year checked off the M20, M21, or M22 manual four-speed. Wrote the editors at *Car Life:* "With the fantastic selection of optional engines,

The four-barrel 302 in the 1969 Z28 still boasted a conservative rating of 290 horsepower. The rubber seal around the open element air cleaner was part of the fresh air system that was standard on the Z28 and optional on other Camaros. Mike Mueller

Starting in 1967, Don Yenko began swapping out 396-ci Chevrolet big-blocks in favor of 427 V-8s for his special Camaros. These fine musclecars were engineered by Dick Harrel. Eventually, the demand for the 427 Camaro exceeded Yenko's ability to supply. To help meet the demand, Yenko discussed the problem with Chevrolet, and Chevrolet agreed to build the 427 Camaro under Central Office Production Order (COPO) 9561 beginning in 1969. David Newhardt

gearboxes, rear axles, suspension, comfort packages, trim groups, etc., etc., etc., there's no reason why a buyer can't be ecstatically happy with his Camaro. These cars are put together quite nicely—only minor signs of sloppiness or poor workmanship in any we've driven. We also consider the Camaro's styling quite attractive, and altogether it's a car that can easily become an extension of anybody's personality or ego."

Sales picked up somewhat for 1968 but not as much as Chevrolet had hoped. A total of 235,147 Camaros rolled off dealers' lots that year. Sales of Rally Sports and Super Sports dropped that year, but incredibly, sales of the Z28 zoomed from 602 in 1967 to nearly 7,200 units in 1968. All in all, it was a good year for the Camaro.

Chevrolet had been at work in the styling studio to spruce up the Camaro's looks for 1969. The most noticeable changes were the speed creases that

Yenko's big-block Camaro buyers often ordered specially available Yenko options. Among the most popular were the Atlas aluminum, five-spoke, mag-type wheels that featured a special Yenko center cap. The wheels gave the Camaro an even more intimidating look on the street, and performed admirably while racing at the strip. The special Yenko striping treatment was standard. David Newhardt

The 1969 Yenko Camaro also received COPO 9737—the Sports Car Conversion Kit. The kit included a 140-mile-per-hour speedometer, E70x15 tires on rally wheels (if the Atlas wheels were not ordered), and a hefty 1-inch-diameter front anti-sway bar. David Newhardt

bled off the tops of the wheel openings. More subtle changes included the front grille and rear taillight facia and the appearance louvers in front of the rear wheel openings. Later in the model year, Chevrolet introduced a functional cowl induction hood. This was standard on the very limited ZL-1 Camaros powered by the all-aluminum 427 V-8, the iron-block 427 COPO Camaros, the Z10 Indy pace car coupe and Z11 Indy pace car convertible, and optional on other performance models. The option code for this hood was ZL2 and it cost $79; over 10,000 were checked off on the option sheet.

The Z28 continued to be a perennial test car favorite with the enthusiast magazines in 1969. Both single four-barrel and optional dual four-barrel Zs were tested, but in terms of straight-line performance they were practically identical. *Car Life* tested the eight-barrel Z28, and the editors complained of the difficulty in getting the car off the line. Until the radical solid lifter camshaft got above 4,000 rpm, it was slow going—after that the car took off like a scalded cat. Nevertheless, quarter-mile times were less than impressive for that reason, managing only 94 miles per hour in 15.12 seconds for the quarter-mile. This virtual race engine naturally was out of its element on the street. *Road Test* got behind the wheel of the single four-barrel 302 Z28 with four-speed manual. Performance was within tenths of a second to 60 miles per hour and in the quarter-mile compared to the dual four-barrel Z. The editors were enthusiastic with their test car. "Is it a practical car for everyday use, then?" the *Road Test* editors asked. "We'd answer this with a definite yes, qualified only by stating that the Z28 is definitely a 'man's car' and not for little old ladies, of whatever gender."

This year proved to be the best sales year yet for the Camaro, with 243,085 sold. The high sales were due in part to an extension of the production year by several months to permit a delayed introduction of the all-new Camaro in February 1970. Broken down, here are the numbers: 37,773 Rally Sports, 33,980 Super Sports, 19,014 Z28s, and 17,573 convertibles. Of all these, 178,087 Camaros had V-8s and a surprising 65,008 were ordered with the straight-six engine. The popularity of the Camaro continued to grow, and Chevrolet was certain the all-new 1970 Camaro would do even better.

The 427-ci V-8 Yenko/SC was a terror on the streets from Woodward Avenue to Hollywood Boulevard. Most Yenko/SCs saw equal duty racing on the street and on the quarter-mile. With 425 or more horsepower under the hood, the Yenko/SC took home money from the street and trophies from the strip. David Newhardt

Owners of other musclecars ignored the Yenko/SC graphic (at their peril). Of course, owners of 426 Hemis, Boss 429s, and similar heavy iron were worthy contenders to the power of the Yenko/SC. This indeed was the musclecar golden age. David Newhardt

CHAPTER 2

STYLE, ELEGANCE, AND MUSCLE

1 9 7 0 – 1 9 7 3

Shortly after the Camaro was launched, the Chevrolet engineering and design studios set to work on the next-generation car. The first-generation Camaro was a crash program and with any new program, engineers always wish they had more time. With the second generation car, the division was committed to improving it and making it superior to the original version and to the Mustang as well. At the time GM felt that any car exterior could go only three years before a major redesign. Division Manager Pete Estes was determined to make the next generation Camaro an absolute stunner, with greatly improved handling, and power in the performance versions to rival any other car on the road. That sounded like a tall order, but this was Chevrolet Division.

Of course, Chevrolet had to look around and see what other manufacturers were doing, as well as other GM divisions. The Mustang was the sales leader for this particular niche. Plymouth had its

Chevrolet launched the second-generation Camaro in 1970. The 350-ci LT1 solid lifter V-8 now powered the Z28. The Super Scoop fresh air hood was a casualty of the new body style. Chevrolet chose not to offer a convertible. Mike Mueller.

second-generation Barracuda. And of course, there was the Pontiac Firebird.

Pontiac had come to the table after the Camaro, when Pontiac Division was given the nod to build its own F-car—GM's designation for pony car. That was a good decision by GM, because Pontiac was very much the performance division at General Motors. After all, the GTO had by now become legend. The 1967 GTO was turning heads everywhere it went and it had the power to back up the image. Pontiac had a completely restyled GTO that would make its debut in 1968, and Chevrolet knew that. In fact all the GM divisions had performance cars: Buick with its GS Skylarks, Pontiac with its GTO and Firebird, Oldsmobile with its 4-4-2, and Chevrolet with its Camaro, and, of course, Corvette. Yet the market was by no means glutted. Performance was hot, and hot styling fueled sales.

The new Camaro body drew rave reviews from the editors, and the car scored high marks for its performance and handling. The spoiler on the 1970 Z28 had a lower profile than that on the Pontiac Trans Am. Mike Mueller

Camaro's European Influence

Against this backdrop, Chevrolet began work on the next Camaro. In the late 1960s, Italian GTs were the most desirable cars on the market. Lamborghini was marketing its sleek 350 GT, Maserati its 3500 GT, and Ferrari several Berlinettas. These Italian makes would have a profound effect on the new generation Camaro. Bill Mitchell, vice president of design for GM, felt these cars literally embodied the style, performance, and love of the high-performance car. He intended to focus and direct the Chevrolet studio toward that end.

In fact, work had progressed so dramatically on the second generation Camaro during 1967 that by January 1968, a full-scale fiberglass static model was finished that very closely resembled the eventual production car. Many, many clay models preceded this stage, however, displaying all manner of body design and roof configurations. One of the key decisions was the elimination of the rear quarter windows. To achieve this, the doors had to be longer. This had the added benefit of easier entry and exit for rear seat passengers.

Perhaps the most important styling element of the whole car was the front end. What evolved was a tall, pointed grille opening with a split bumper, single headlights with round parking lights inboard of the headlights. The traditional center-mounted license plate location often dictated the shape of the front grille; Haga's studio developed an offset license plate mounting location to the left of the grille opening and below the small bumper so as not to alter the desired aesthetic goal. Mitchell approved it. The studio then developed a refinement to this design with a slim, full-width bumper and the parking lamps in a rectangular configuration below the bumper.

A convertible was proposed for the second-generation Camaro and one was modeled in clay. However, sales of the convertible amounted to only 10 percent of total Camaro production. The cost of tooling—and engineering—a convertible in light of these production numbers killed the idea. Some in Chevrolet engineering sighed in relief because the dreaded convertible cowl shake had never been satisfactorily resolved. The new Camaro would not have that problem.

The interior of the new car would also be radically different. Mitchell encouraged George Angersbach's No. 2 Interior Studio to explore much more sculpted shapes in the design of the dash, door panels, console, and even the seats. Mitchell wanted more emphasis on driver instrumentation with dials instead of warning lights. GM was making the move away from stamped metal for dashboards toward crushable high-density, foam-backed molded plastic, for safety reasons. Doing this also allowed more design flexibility to achieve the sculpted shape of the dash the studio was pursuing.

The new Camaro design presented engineering challenges that resulted in a constant battle with the design studio. The low cowl created a host of problems for heating and air conditioning ducting, not to mention packaging of the instrumentation, access to wiring, and glovebox design. Space was at such a premium, the heating, ventilation, and air conditioning

(HVAC) engineers made urgent requests to raise the cowl height. This was vehemently opposed by the design studio. The correspondingly low hoodline put limitations on engine location within the chassis. The engine could go only so low in the stub-frame, which was reengineered for the second-generation car. This issue of the low cowl and hoodline was a crucial aesthetic baseline because it dictated the main stylistic element of the car, running from the top of the headlights, along the front fenders to the door sill, and continuing onto the rear fenderline, terminating at the lip of the trunk lid. If this was raised, the car would look too tall and heavy. Design won out after many battles. Mitchell remained firm and backed up Haga's studio.

Interestingly, Chevrolet also looked very strongly at building a Khamback design which harkened back to the glory days of the famous Nomad of the mid-1950s. It was, essentially, a two-door wagon. The Chevrolet studio came up with several such designs incorporating the new body style. In the end, it was voted down because it seemed to conflict with the sporting nature of the Camaro. Some suggested

Z28 identification appeared on the front grille, front fenders, and rear spoiler. Less than 9,000 Z28s were built in 1970, due to a late introduction. Mike Mueller

A choice of three different four-speed manual transmissions could be ordered on the new Z28. For the first time, a buyer could order the Turbo HydraMatic transmission in the "Z," thanks to the torque generated by the LT1 V-8. Mike Mueller

"sportwagen" would establish a new niche within a niche. It was not approved for production. There would be only one body style for the new Camaro—the Sport Coupe.

New Chassis Engineering

There was a formidable team lined up to ensure that the new Camaro's structure and suspension offered superb ride, handling, and safety. Don McPherson was now passenger car chief engineer, Charlie Rubley was staff engineer, and reporting to him was Bob Dorn, who was in charge of Camaro chassis engineering. GM wanted to minimize the number of unique suspension components across its lines, moving toward a "corporate" front suspension with common unequal-length upper and lower control arms and other front suspension and steering components. This was fine for the full-size and midsize GM cars, but in the Camaro this posed a challenge, in light of the big-block V-8 that would continue to be offered. In addition, the steering column was engineered to be collapsible and the steering box relocated from behind, to in front of, the front axle line.

The task then fell to Dorn to ensure the "generic" front suspension was engineered with the specific camber and toe, coupled with the steering gear ratio, to achieve the quick steering response wanted in the Camaro. This suspension also needed to accept a range of specific spring rates, shock absorber rates, and antiroll bars to tune handling based on the engine in the car—from the straight-six to the big-block V-8. With the rear suspension, the best balance of

ride and handling control was achieved using multi-leaf rear springs.

The second-generation Camaro exhibited improved handling. The redesigned suspension helped with this, as did a broader stance, from a 1.5-inch wider front track and a 0.5-inch wider rear track. Wheelbase remained the same at 108 inches. This Camaro received a standard 0.93-inch front antisway bar. Chevrolet engineers developed a performance handling package, with the eventual option code F41, that kept the same base car spring rates but included heavy-duty shocks, a larger diameter front antisway bar, and the addition of a rear antisway bar.

Engineering and testing staff spent many months at GM's Milford, Michigan, proving grounds evaluating and improving the new Camaro. Simultaneously, the car was developed to go racing, or at least engineered so as to be effectively worked on by professional racers for SCCA, drag racing, even a hoped-for NASCAR class. However, all this development testing took time—more time than general manager John DeLorean wanted. He wanted and

had planned for the new Camaro to be introduced in the fall of 1969 as a 1970 model. All the reports coming back from engineering and manufacturing were saying the same thing: the deadline to establish the new production line in the summer of 1969 could not be met.

DeLorean met with all the leads on the Camaro program to nail down when the car could go into production. With the engineering programs completed and long, lead tooling procured, it would be February 1970 before the car would roll into Chevrolet dealers. It was decided it would be best to introduce the new Camaro as a 1970-1/2 model, rather than a very early 1971 model. It was felt that this later idea proved unworkable in terms of new vehicle registration and would have caused confusion in the market. The 1969 Camaro would continue in production the additional number of months necessary before the production line switched over for the all-new Camaro.

Facing the Competition

Even before Chevrolet had the long-awaited opportunity to put the 1970-1/2 Camaro into

Camaro Sport Coupe

Camaro Sport Coupe with RS Equipment

When Chevrolet introduced the second-generation Camaro on February 26, 1970, the new Camaro was billed as a 1970 1/2 model. The Sport Coupe is shown on the left and an RS optioned Sport Coupe, with its unique front end, is on the right.

showrooms and on dealers' lots, there was new competition to make the pony car market even more hotly contested. Ford had unveiled an all-new Mustang for 1969, and it was turning heads wherever it went. For 1970, the Mustang was refined aesthetically, going from a four-headlight to a two-headlight arrangement, which many said improved the sleek fastback Mustang's looks even more. Ford fired its big guns by offering the Boss 302, Boss 429, and Cobra Jet Mustangs in a withering salvo of performance. But that's not all Chevrolet faced.

Chrysler Corporation also stepped into the pony car ring. Plymouth had been selling its Barracuda

since 1964, but for the first and second generation it was a car in search of an identity. All that vanished with the 1970 Barracuda and its performance derivative, the 'Cuda. It was judged by a number of enthusiast magazines to be the best-looking pony car on the market. And the 'Cuda was available with either standard high-performance 383, six-barrel 440, or the elephant engine itself: the 426 Hemi. Dodge Division launched its Challenger on a similar but not identical platform with a slightly longer wheelbase. It had the same powertrain options. And—here's the kicker—both the Dodge Challenger and Plymouth 'Cuda were available as convertibles.

Even the No. 4 car maker, American Motors, had its pony car offering to cause Chevrolet even more concern. Its two-seater AMX was introduced in 1968. In 1970 it received a mild styling rework. Its high-performance 390-ci V-8 made the AMX a good performer on the street, but in terms of sales numbers it was not a threat.

Against this embarrassment of riches in pony car offerings, Chevrolet put the new Camaro on sale on February 13, 1970. The division was supremely confident in the new Camaro and the segment of the car-buying market it was appealing to. The first-generation Camaro had achieved the highest percentage of buyers 25 years old and younger—over 50 percent. One in four of all Camaro buyers were women. Manager John DeLorean in particular, and Chevrolet in general, saw the Camaro as the car

to establish Chevrolet brand loyalty. The Camaro was not an end in itself, but a means to an end—that end being satisfied Chevrolet buyers who would move on to other models as they grew older or established families. The Chevelle and full-size Chevrolet were logical choices here, but those wanting performance in a more sophisticated package could go for the Corvette.

Price-wise, the new Camaro was a very afford-able car. The Sport Coupe with 250-ci six-cylinder was $2,749. The V-8 Sport Coupe with 307-ci V-8 ran $2,849. Nearly 35,000 buyers opted for the 250-horsepower 350-ci V-8 and it was a bargain at only $31.60. Once again, performance and appear-ance could be had in two distinct packages: the SS and the Z28. The RPO (Regular Production Option) for the SS package was Z27, but this never caught on with buyers. The SS option cost $289.65 and included the

The 1970 1/2 Camaro Sport Coupe with standard 250-ci six-cylinder engine had a base list price of $2,749, and the Sport Coupe V-8 was only $2,859. Here was style, fuel-economy, and affordability all in one package.

The big-block V-8 continued to be available in the Camaro through the 1972 model year. Advertised displacement was 396 cubic inches, but actual displacement from a slightly larger bore put it at 402 cubic inches. All big-blocks were assembled at GM's famed Tonawanda, New York, engine plant. Here, mighty big-blocks are being stored and await shipment to various GM assembly plants. Chevrolet

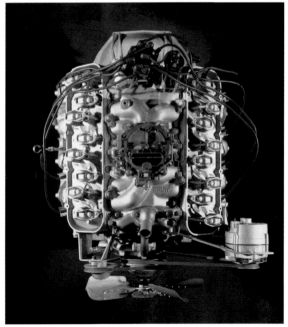

With the valve covers removed, the staggered juxtaposition of intake and exhaust rocker arms are evident. In 1972, the last year the 396/402 big-block appeared in the Camaro SS, net horsepower dropped down to 240. Note the thin wall casting employed for the valve cover seat. Chevrolet

300-horsepower 350 high-performance V-8 bolted to either the Turbo HydraMatic automatic transmission or one of the four-speed manual transmissions. The Z28 option listed for $572.95. It featured the new LT1 V-8—churning out 350 horsepower—basically the same engine available in the Corvette with a slightly lower rated output so as not to embarrass America's "only sportscar."

The Rally Sport option (Z22) allowed Camaro buyers to achieve a different look for their cars. Instead of the full-width chrome front bumper with parking lights below the bumper, the front end of the Rally Sport featured a resilient plastic surround on the leading edge with rubber-tipped vertical center bar, a blacked-out grille, small bumpers below each headlight, concealed windshield wipers, and other features. The Rally Sport option could be ordered on the Camaro SS or the Z28; Rally Sport identification was deleted when the SS or the Z28 option was

ordered. Naturally, the hottest Camaro was the Z28, and for 1970 it had a brand-new standard high-performance V-8.

The LT-1 350-ci V-8

In the battle for musclecar loyalty during the late 1960s and early 1970s, not all pavement pounders were powered by big-block V-8s. In fact, some of the best street screamers were powered by high-winding small-blocks. Chevrolet's 350-ci LT-1, introduced for 1970, was the pinnacle of hi-po Chevy small-block development during the musclecar golden age.

Notwithstanding the problems the 295-horsepower 350 encountered when first released, Chevrolet made the decision to build a truly high-performance 350 to take over the performance mantle once carried by the 365-horsepower and 375-horsepower 327 V-8s. This engine was to be built without compromise, fitted with premium parts throughout, and

would be offered in the Camaro Z28 and the Corvette for 1970.

Chevrolet engineers started with the company's rugged cast-iron 350 V-8 engine block and added four-bolt main bearing caps. The standard nodular cast-iron crankshaft was replaced by a new forged steel unit. As always, the connecting rods were drop-forged steel. The forged aluminum 11.0:1 pistons made by TRW were essentially identical to those used in the L-46 350-horsepower 350 V-8. The LT-1 mechanical camshaft was designed with an intake duration of 317 degrees, an exhaust duration of 346 degrees and an overlap of 96 degrees, 3 seconds. Lift for both intake and exhaust was 0.458 inch.

The cylinder heads were cast iron and had many features that first appeared on the cylinder heads that came on the fuel-injected 327 previously offered in the Corvette. This included 2.02-inch diameter intake valves, 1.60-inch diameter exhaust valves, and

Chevrolet produced several design studies of a Khamback Camaro for the second-generation car. Although the design was inspired by the two-door Nomad of the late 1950s, GM voted it down as being out of character for the Camaro.

a 64-cc combustion chamber. In addition, the cylinder head was machined for screw-in rocker arm studs and featured hardened steel pushrod guide plates.

The induction system included a cast-aluminum high-riser dual-plane intake manifold, plus a Holley 780-cubic feet per minute (cfm) four-barrel carburetor with 1.686-inch diameter primary and secondary throttle bores. In the 1970 Z28, the LT-1 was fitted with a dual-snorkle air cleaner. In the Corvette that year, an open-element air filter with chrome air filter cover was used; this is the setup most often seen in factory photos of the LT-1. Aesthetically, this very special engine merited and received approval for a set of striking finned cast-aluminum valve covers that made the statement that Chevrolet viewed this engine as its finest small-block to date.

As installed in the Corvette, the LT-1 was rated at 370 horsepower at 6,000 rpm with 380 ft-lb of torque at 4,000 rpm. In deference to the Corvette, the 1970 Z28 with the standard LT-1 engine was rated at 360 horsepower at 6,000 rpm and having the same torque rating. There was no mechanical difference between the LT-1 available in the Corvette and standard in the Z28. Since this rating was achieved on the dyno, no explanation was forthcoming from Chevrolet to explain the difference. It may only have been on paper.

The Z28 option, which included the LT-1 as part of the package, listed for $572.95. However, there were mandatory options that had to be purchased if the Z28 option was checked off. These additional options included either one of the heavy-duty four-speed manual transmissions ($205.95–$232.35) or

The long-cherished ability of hot cars to pick up girls proved a suitable theme to use in Z28 advertising. According to this ad, the progression from a hot bike to a hot car separated the men from their toys.

Chevrolet wisely kept all prospective Z28 buyers within the scope of its advertising for 1970. Being married with children was no deterrent to the family man wanting a sports car, thanks to the four-place seating of the Z28.

the Turbo HydraMatic automatic transmission ($200.65), G80 Posi-Traction rear axle ($44.25), and power brakes ($47.40), which came with front discs and rear drums.

The Press Weighs In

The solid lifter LT-1 really was a superb engine, and magazine editors were eager to get their hands on a 1970 Z28 or LT-1. Attempting to determine the difference between the LT-1 Corvette and Z28, *Car & Driver* conducted a side-by-side test. Both cars were equipped with four-speed manual transmissions and limited-slip 4.11 differentials. The Corvette

reached 60 miles per hour in 6.7 seconds and covered the quarter-mile in 14.5 seconds doing 99.5 miles per hour. The Z28 reached 60 miles per hour in 6.7 seconds and tripped the timing lights in 14.6 seconds doing 98.3 miles per hour. It was virtually a dead heat, and the Z28 cost $2,000 less than the voluptuous Corvette.

Car Life also tested the 1970 Z28 for its May 1970 issue. This car came with the Turbo HydraMatic automatic tranny—a first for the Z28 because the previous 302 didn't have the torque or low-speed driveability compatible with Chevy's automatic transmission. The 350-ci LT-1 solved this problem. Times were nearly

Joel Rosen of the Baldwin-Motion Performance Group on Long Island continued to offer the biggest of the big-blocks—the 454—in his specially modified Camaros. His Phase III Camaros became legends in their own time and collectibles in later years. These two ads marked the end of the big-block Camaro era prior to the advent of catalytic converters in 1975.

identical to the four-speed model, reaching 60 miles per hour in 6.5 seconds and buzzing the Chrondecks in 14.5 seconds at 98.79 miles per hour.

The editors at *Hot Rod* also tested a manual Z28, this time at California's Riverside Raceway. This was a great venue for the Z28 and the editors felt all-around performance on the Riverside track to be very good, but they were somewhat disappointed the Z didn't record quarter-mile times in the low 14s. This could be fixed by disemboweling the Z28 of its less-than-ideal exhaust system and installing tube headers and a good dual-exhaust system. Many Z28 owners did this and succeeded in seeing the far side of 100 miles per hour in their assaults on the quarter-mile.

Perhaps the most demanding automotive editors on the face of the planet are those at *Road & Track* magazine. Ever since its inception, it was heavily prejudiced toward imported cars and rarely tested American automobiles. By the late 1960s, the editors had begun to warm up to Detroit's offerings. They were most eager to test the 1970-1/2 Camaro and give it an objective evaluation. Rather than drive the Z28, they tested the Rally Sport with 300-horsepower 350 engine in SS trim. And they loved it. The editors raved about the new Camaro, calling it "the first serious effort since the 1963 Corvette to create a real American GT." Their conclusion was even stronger: "We'll have to say it's the best American car we've ever driven, and more importantly, it's one of the most satisfying cars for all-around use we've ever driven."

Incredibly, despite all the accolades from the magazines, its handsome new body, excellent powertrain offerings, and the best handling ever, sales of the Camaro took a dramatic nosedive. The new Plymouth Barracuda and Dodge Challenger had a significant impact, especially the convertible models. So did the many other makes and models that offered eye-catching styling and any level of performance you wanted. The new Camaro was in a very fierce market, as Chevrolet found out.

With the second-generation Camaro, Chevrolet achieved its hoped-for objective *vis-a-vis* the Mustang. By April of 1970, Camaro sales initially surpassed those of the Mustang. Sales of the Camaro were so heavy, a third shift was added to the Norwood, Ohio, assembly plant. But sales started to slow with so many other desirable cars to chose from, and the emergence of an economic recession. Camaro sales

for the 1970 model year totaled 121,901, roughly half the sales of the previous year. Ford regained its lead, selling over 170,000 Mustangs in 1970. Clearly the late introduction of the new Camaro hurt sales. A total of 8,733 Z28s were sold. The Z28 proved a much better seller than its big-block cousin, the SS 396 Camaro. Only 1,864 SS 396 Camaros with the 350-horse L34 big-block were sold in 1970. A mere 600 SS Camaros with the 375-horsepower L78 396 left dealer showrooms that year. The big-block insurance surcharge really kicked the stuffing out of hoped-for sales. Thus, the LT-1 powered Z28 proved to be a smart engineering *and* marketing move.

Spitting into the Wind—1971

It is inevitable that when a car manufacturer introduces an all-new car in a given year, the next production year will show little if any change. Why should there be? Chevrolet had invested so much engineering and styling effort in the new Camaro, only minor refinements were deemed necessary. Actually, there were significant changes, due to government regulations.

The first bad news started with a United Auto Workers (UAW) strike that idled the Camaro production line from the middle of September 1970 until just before Thanksgiving—a total of 70 days. When the 1971 Camaros finally did start arriving on dealer lots,

Chevrolet continued to appeal to the family man who wanted a brand new 1972 Camaro SS. The campaign was actually quite clever. This ad emphasized the Camaro SS as a sports car with a back seat. Due to insurance premiums, not many took Chevrolet up on the offer. Only 970 big-block 1972 Camaro SS' were ordered.

Type LT. For those who want a little more Camaro.

Choice of 5 luxury interiors: 3 cloth, 2 all-vinyl.

Variable-ratio power steering, LT insignia.

14 x 7 Rally Wheels. White stripe tires available.

Twin sport mirrors, driver's remote controlled.

New Camaro Type LT. L for Luxury, T for Touring. Type LT is for those who want a little more Camaro than the basic Sport Coupe. Yes, everything mentioned is standard equipment with Camaro Type LT.

Front disc brakes, finned rear drum brakes.

Special LT instrumentation, tachometer, ammeter, temperature gauge, electric clock.

LT Engine, our Turbo-Fire 350-2 V8.

Chevrolet. Building a better way to see the U.S.A.

Take a second to buckle up. It could save a lifetime.

Chevrolet dropped the Camaro SS at the end of 1972. In 1973 the division introduced the Type LT, which stood for Luxury Touring, signaling the de-emphasis of performance. The division sold over 32,000 that year.

shoppers did not see anything strikingly different from 1970—and that was good. The second-generation Camaro was a superb styling statement and would prove to be a very enduring design. There was virtually no change outside from bumper to bumper. There were refinements to the seating and other minor aesthetic changes. The greatest change to the

Camaro—and practically all cars for 1971—took place under the hood.

The days of high-performance high-compression V-8s were about to come to an end. Automobile emissions regulations promulgated by the Environmental Protection Agency (EPA) would force manufacturers to lower compression ratios and reengineer their engines to run first on low-lead and then lead-free gasoline. Chevrolet high-performance development engineer Bill Howell was there to witness the transition.

"Nineteen seventy was the last year of high-performance, high-compression ratios," says Howell. "Across the board, the corporation went low compression. Engine development virtually stopped on the hardware because the stuff was so good at higher compression ratios, that when you took the loads off of it, you didn't have to do any durability testing. The testing was now concentrated on the emissions area. They took all the dollars out of our engine development and put it into emissions development, because each year the emissions laws got tougher."

"For 1971," recalls Joe Bertsch, first-line supervisor of the V-8 engine design group at the time, "our big development program was the revision of the compression ratios on all the engines. That was a relatively simple program, to be quite truthful. So many of the problems we had worked on prior to that with the high-compression engines went away. On the 327 and 350 high-compression versions, we had problems with bulkhead cracking and the cylinder wall cracking intermittently. Dropping compression ratios on the engines really dispensed with just about all the mechanical development problems."

The lowered compression ratios were reflected in the lower horsepower ratings for 1971. The compression ratio for the LT-1 was dropped two full points, to 9.0:1. The mechanical camshaft's specifications, however, remained unchanged. Basically, there was a 10 percent drop in horsepower and torque. The engine was now rated at 330 horsepower at 5,600 rpm with 360 ft-lb of torque at 4,000 rpm. The SAE net horsepower rating was 275 horsepower. *Motor Trend* tested a 1971 Z28 with automatic transmission and 3.73 differential. The car reached 60 miles per hour in a disappointing 7.6 seconds and covered the quarter-mile in 15.4 seconds at 90 miles per hour. Sales of the Z28 were nearly halved to 4,862 cars. Nevertheless, the *Road & Track* editors remained

impressed enough to cite the 1971 Camaro as one of the Ten Best Cars in the World.

A 400-ci Small-Block for Camaro?

As early as 1970, Vince Piggins had anticipated the performance drop that would be experienced by all of Chevrolet's engines following the drop in compression ratios. He wrote a memorandum to Don McPherson in March of that year suggesting a 400-ci small-block V-8 to go into the Z28. Chevrolet had already introduced the 400-ci small-block V-8 in its full-size passenger cars and the engine had a distinct plus—four-bolt main bearing caps. This was the largest small-block Chevrolet ever built and it presented considerable challenges. How it almost ended up in Camaros is an interesting story.

How did the 400-ci V-8 come about? "I'll just give you one word: politics," says engineer Dick Keinath. "The 400 was a very political animal. I think it all boiled down to a feud between Mr. Knudsen and Mr. Cole. The big-block was all done when Mr. Knudsen was general manager. Mr. Cole never liked the big-block engines. He realized that there was a need to keep the large-block displacement around, but he thought he could do it by using his small-block as the basis for it. And that's the politics of it."

Despite Cole's optimism, expanding the bores to 4.125 inches and the stoke to 3.75 inches created a host of problems. To achieve the required bore, the cylinder walls now had to be siamesed; there would be no space between them for coolant to flow. Another problem was increased oil consumption.

In 1973, the Z28 enjoyed a record sales year. Despite high insurance premiums, 11,574 Z28s were sold that year. Bob Routt bought this car for $3,695 and still owns it today. The car underwent a total restoration that was completed in March 2000. This car ranks as one of the finest 1973 Z28s in North America. **Anthony Young**

55

With the larger bores closer to the cylinder head bolts, there was some distortion of the area near the head bolts when they were torqued down, and oil consumption rose as a result. Still, these problems were overcome, and it gave the small-block new life in the face of imminent lower compression ratios.

And why the move to four-bolt main bearing caps? "The Mk IV big-block engines were very expensive and heavy," says Joe Bertsch, assistant staff engineer in the V-8 engine group at the time. "As I remember, there was a 150-pound weight differential between the small-block V-8 and the Mk IV. The 400 was just an effort to get the maximum displacement possible out of the small-block V-8. The engine had to have the bores siamesed and you couldn't make the bores any larger because, with a 4-1/8-inch bore, that only left 0.28 inch between the cylinders, a very minimal dimension to seal the head gaskets at that point.

"As I remember," says Bertsch, "the 350 truck engine and the high-compression 350 had four-bolt mains. Putting four-bolt mains on the 400 was pretty much a carry-over of that practice. The four-bolt mains

were primarily a fix introduced on the engine to increase crankshaft durability during the development of the nodular iron crankshaft. The reason was cost. At that point, that was worth between five and six dollars in cost savings per crank."

It was Vince Piggins' hope that a 400-ci small-block with 800-cubic feet per minute (cfm) Holley carburetor, appropriate hydraulic camshaft, and high numerical axle ratio would help to keep the low-compression Z28 of 1971 a good performer. However, the plan was turned down because of concern for unlimited rpm applications in manual transmission-equipped cars. The 400 was only approved for automatic transmission applications, and there would not be a high enough volume to justify offering it in the Z28.

Despite this, both *Car & Driver* and *Road & Track* had glowing things to say about the 1971 Camaro. The 1971 Readers' Choice Poll in *Car & Driver* unanimously selected the 1971 Camaro as the best car in its class—pony car—by a margin of two-to-one over the Mustang. The editors of *Road &*

Track selected the 1971 Camaro SS 350 as one of the Ten Best Cars in the World. It was the only American-made car to make the list, which included the Mercedes Benz 300SEL 6.3, Porsche 911, and Ferrari 365 GTB/4 Daytona. Total Camaro production for 1971 was 114,630.

Downshifting the Camaro

The performance era in the early 1970s was coming to a close. The manufacturers were getting hammered from all sides to design cars to meet government standards for emissions, crash-worthiness, and interior safety. Nevertheless, the Camaro for 1972 fortunately continued aesthetically unchanged. Camaro enthusiasts argued, "Why change perfection?"

Inflation in the United States in the early 1970s was very low, so car prices changed little, if at all. In December 1971 the automobile excise tax was repealed and dropped from the total vehicle price, so prices for the Camaro were better than ever. For example, the base list price for the V-8 Sport Coupe was only $2,819.70. Interestingly, Chevrolet continued to offer a six-cylinder Sport Coupe. Few of the 4,821 built that year were actually ordered by buyers; they were built and shipped to dealers to have on the lot to advertise the lowest possible price. Still, fuel efficiency was of concern to some Camaro buyers, and the trusty 250-ci six was built for them.

As Chevrolet struggled to meet ever-tightening emissions, LT-1 performance slipped further for 1972, with a new net rating of 255 horsepower.

The second-generation Z28 featured the most graceful lines and some of the best styling of the musclecar era; perfection was in the details. This is why this 1973 Z28 still turns heads today. After the extensive restoration, Routt chose only to show the car—its days as a daily driver are over.
Anthony Young

Sales of the Z28 dropped further, to 2,575 units. All across the performance car landscape, taps was being sounded. LT-1 production ended in 1972. Chevrolet's other performance Camaro, the SS, continued for another year but it too suffered from the decompression blues. The low-compression 350 offered in the Z27 Super Sport package was rated at 200 net horsepower. The optional LS3 396 (actual displacement was 402 cubic inches; Chevrolet kept the original displacement numbers as a legacy) was rated at 240 horsepower.

In April 1972, the UAW stuck again—literally. The Camaro and Firebird assembly line in the Norwood, Ohio, plant again fell silent. That wasn't Camaro's only problem. Bumper standards would take effect for 1973, and would require 1974 models to sustain a 5-mile per hour impact without damage. Engineering ran the cost and it was alarming. Also, no one had any idea the UAW strike would last 171 days—nearly half a year! As the strike dragged on for months and the specter of prohibitive tooling costs for the mandated bumpers loomed overhead, there was very serious talk of canceling the Camaro. Production did resume at the end of September, but there was no time to finish the cars in the plant as 1972 models, so they were scrapped. During the strike, Chevrolet had been at work getting everything it could lined up for the 1973 Camaro. By the end of the 1972 model year, only 68,651 Camaros had been sold. Fortunately, sales of practically all the other Chevrolet models set records. Overall, Chevrolet was in good shape.

Several things saved the Camaro from extinction. Bob Dorn had become chief engineer on the Camaro and he, with his team of engineers, worked to engineer bumpers for the 1973 model that appeared unchanged, but were strong enough to survive the low-speed barrier test with affordable tooling cost. Also, Chevrolet general manager John DeLorean and

The interior was painstakingly restored and looks as new as the day Routt received it in March 1973. The four-speed manual transmission was not the only way to go, but for many Z28 owners, it was the best way. The high-winding small-block 350-ci V-8, coupled with the four-speed Hurst shifter, was the perfect high-performance combination for aggressive driving. **Anthony Young**

chief engineer Alex Mair went to bat for the Camaro on the 14th floor of the GM building in downtown Detroit. They argued to the GM board that to cancel the Camaro would be a mistake, as Ford had no plans to cancel the Mustang. They presented data that the 1974 model could be engineered to withstand the tougher 5-mile per hour bumper standard without radically altering the car's looks and with an acceptable tooling cost. Were it not for leadership like this, the Camaro might have become extinct.

Camaro buffs were relieved when the 1973 models were introduced on September 21. The rumors of the Camaro's demise had proven false, but few outside Chevrolet knew how close the car came to a premature end. On the 1973 cars Chevrolet made a greater effort to offer packages for the Camaro as opposed to a smorgasbord of options. One of these new packages was the Type LT, which stood for "Lusso Turismo," or Luxury Tourer. It came standard with a 145-horsepower 350-ci V-8, special exterior trim and identification, and unique interior appointments. This placed the Type LT near the top of the Camaro line-up, with the six-cylinder and base eight-cylinder Camaro below it, and the optional Z28 above it.

In 1973, the hydraulic lifter L82 was introduced to replace the solid lifter LT-1. Power dropped slightly from 255 to 245 horsepower. This engine received a cast-iron intake manifold and Holley carburetor. With one of the four-speed manual transmissions and a performance axle ratio, the Z28 was still an enjoyable car for performance-minded owners to drive. The 402-ci "396" was not offered in 1973, and the Z27 SS option was also dropped. Performance was in decline, hit hard by high insurance premiums, ever-tightening emissions standards, and manufacturer preoccupation with other regulatory concerns. With nearly 97,000 Camaros sold that year, the 1973 Camaro was relatively unencumbered of government-mandated equipment. Soon the heavy hand of the federal government would drastically alter the shape and character of Chevrolet's pony car.

In 1973, hydraulic valve lifters replaced the solid lifters in the LT1. This made it possible for Chevrolet to offer air conditioning in the Z28 for the first time. A new Holley carburetor was fitted to an iron intake manifold that replaced the aluminum unit. The engine was rated at 245 net horsepower. **Anthony Young**

With the fat Wide Oval spare tire consuming much of the trunk, there wasn't much room for luggage in the 1973 Z28. Soft-sided luggage was a definite plus in this car. Even the jack and related pieces received the restoration treatment. **Anthony Young**

THE MELLOWED MUSCLECAR

1974 – 1977

I n the mid-1970s, the Camaro would enter a ne
era. The Camaro's engineering and even i
appearance would be driven not by the market, n
by Chevrolet, but by regulations issued by the U.
government. The concern about automobile emi
sions was really nothing new. In 1955, the Air Poll
tion Control Act was passed by Congress, authorizir
the Public Health Service to conduct research and pr
vide technical assistance. Five years later, Congres
focused attention on the automobile with the Aut
motive Pollution Control Act, which required the surgec
general to examine the automobile air pollution prol
lem. In 1963, the Clean Air Act was enacted, followe
by the Motor Vehicle Pollution Control Act in 1965, th
first piece of legislation that would directly affect ca
manufacturers. In 1970, staunch environmentalist

*The 1974 Z28 was something of a milestone because
Chevrolet planned to stop production at the end of
the year. A catalytic converter with a single exhaust
system was required in 1975 to meet EPA-mandated
emissions regulations. With ever-tightening emission
regulations in the future, Chevrolet did not feel it
could build a high-performance Camaro with the
illustrious Z28 name. The division would later
change its mind.* David Newhardt

The new energy-absorbing aluminum bumpers on the 1974 Camaro line increased overall length by 7 inches. The 1974 Z28 is an overlooked collectible because it was the last year of true dual exhaust and still had a respectable 245 net horsepower from the L82 hydraulic lifter under the hood. Sales of the 1974 Z28 actually picked up from the previous year and 13,802 units were sold. David Newhardt

achieved their goal of having a new federal agency handling matters of the environment with the establishment of the Environmental Protection Agency, the EPA.

At first, the most visible pollution control device under the hood was the belt-driven air pump, which injected air into the exhaust stream to reduce unburned hydrocarbons. Most of these pumps were installed on cars destined for California, which maintains pollution standards more stringent than those nationally. The next series of regulations was actually directed at the gasoline companies. The EPA issued rules to reduce the amount of lead in gasoline. Lead was used as a lubricant and antiknock additive. This in turn required manufacturers to lower compression

ratios in order for car engines to run on low-lead gasoline. That happened in 1971. The EPA rules stated lead would have to be eliminated from gasoline in several years.

In addition to the millions of engineering dollars GM would need to reengineer its engines to meet tightening emission controls and run on low-lead or no-lead gasoline, the company faced a gauntlet of regulations on bumper standards, crash protection, rollover standards, and occupant protection. Countless meetings were held in Washington between the car manufacturers and committees in charge of promulgating these regulations to try to slow the pace of implementation. Alarming articles appeared in all the automotive magazines chronicling the challenges by car makers to all the seemingly impossible regulations. The picture the editors painted was that the American automobile was going to change forever.

A Brave New World

For nearly six decades, the American automobile had not drawn the attention of Washington, and car manufacturers pretty much built the cars the way they felt they should be built. Even seatbelts were not standard equipment in most domestic cars until Washington required manufacturers to install them in the 1960s. This euphoria of unfettered manufacturing all came to an end in the 1970s. Like a tidal wave, a staggering array of regulations washed

The 1974 Z28 still presented a street image of performance in the face of declining net horsepower and rising insurance premiums. For about $3,600 you could buy one of the best performance cars built in America. David Newhardt

over car manufacturers and it was no stretch to say even the mighty General Motors and Ford Motor Company struggled to meet them all. Of course, all these regulations had a price, which was passed on to the consumer.

The Camaro had a near-death experience in 1972 due to the extended UAW strike. Nevertheless the 1973 models went on sale right on schedule. But the 1974 models reflected the new world of government regulation of the automobile. The 1974 Camaro displayed new front and rear end styling with full-fledged 5-mile per hour bumpers. Reengineering the Camaro to carry these bumpers did bump up the weight. Still, the bumpers were well integrated into the body design and did not detract too much from the Camaro's handsome lines.

Inside there was evidence of more regulation. Drivers now had to buckle their seatbelts before turning the ignition key would start the car. This was known as the seatbelt-ignition interlock system. Some owners, outraged at this brazen display of Big Brother watching out for them, simply buckled the seatbelt

permanently. The only thing those lap/shoulder belts were going to restrain were the seats themselves. Of course, in the event of a collision, the driver did not get a second chance to reconsider his decision.

The event that had the greatest impact on the American automobile, more than all the government regulations, was the Arab Oil Embargo. In an effort to dramatically boost the price of a barrel of oil, the United Arab Emirates imposed an oil embargo on North America. The embargo began in October 1973 to restrict but not totally stop the flow of crude petroleum to the United States. Gasoline had been averaging 35 cents a gallon, but suddenly prices started rising quickly as demand outstripped supply. Within weeks gas was 70–75 cents a gallon—when it could be bought at all.

The American gasoline companies were forced to restrict deliveries of gasoline to their dealers, and long gas lines were a routine sight around the country. Many dealers limited purchases to a $5 or $10 maximum. States imposed gasoline rationing using the odd/even system in an effort to relieve the long lines.

Few original-condition examples of the 1974 Z28 exist today. Despite the imposition of the aluminum bumpers on the car's extremities, the classic lines of the second-generation Camaro remained undiminished. David Newhardt

A close-up view of the L82 under the hood of the 1974 Z28. Chevrolet still cared enough about the Z to include the cast-aluminum intake manifold and finned aluminum valve covers. Soon the uncluttered engine compartment of the Camaro would be smothered with additional emissions plumbing, valves, and hoses. David Newhardt

The stamped-steel mag-type wheels were a distinctive performance styling cue on the Z28 for most of the 1970s. In the first half of the decade, they were painted a metallic-like argent color. When the Z28 returned in 1977, the wheels were painted to match the body color. David Newhardt

Drivers with license plates ending in an odd number could buy gas on an odd-numbered day only, and drivers with plates ending in an even number could buy gas only on an even-numbered day. Nevertheless, many drivers remember waiting in lines having over 100 cars in the queue.

The Arabs kept the pressure on for weeks, then months. Gasoline was no longer a plentiful commodity, but very precious. Cars with V-8 engines were now called "gas guzzlers" and full-size cars languished on dealers' lots with no buyers. Consumers rushed to snap up compact cars with four- and six-cylinder engines. Volkswagen, Toyota, Honda, and other imported compact car makers started doing a landslide business; many dealers began having extended evening hours to handle the unprecedented demand.

How did the oil crisis affect the Camaro? For one thing, it boosted sales! The Camaro had always been offered with a six-cylinder engine, but these cars had never sold more than a few thousand units. The oil embargo completely changed the equation. Many new car buyers wanted Camaro style with a gas-stingy six under the hood. The Camaro and Firebird had also been built at the Van Nuys, California, plant between 1967 and 1971, besides the Norwood, Ohio, plant. Chevrolet decided to close down the Van Nuys assembly line after 1971 and add a third shift to the Norwood, Ohio, plant. With the demand once again rising for the Camaro, and six-cylinder models in particular, Chevrolet reopened the Van Nuys assembly line for the 1974 model year. Sales of the six-cylinder Camaro Sport Coupe zoomed from just over 3,600 in 1973 to over 22,000 for 1974.

Like a valiant soldier having survived a war intact, the Z28 returned for 1974 to carry the performance torch for one more year. The 350-ci V-8 in the Z28 was rated at 245 net horsepower—still a respectable output and unchanged from 1973. Perhaps some saw the end was near for unrestricted performance, because sales of the Z28 started climbing again and by model year's end, Chevrolet had sold 13,802 Z28s. Nearly 49,000 Type LT Camaros were sold in 1974, but by far the best seller of the Camaro corral was the V-8 Sport Coupe, with 79,835 sales. With a base list price for the Type LT of just over $3,000, it was no wonder the Camaro sold well, embargo or no embargo. Total sales for 1974 numbered 151,008 cars.

The End of Dual Exhaust

For several years, General Motors had been working on the development of a catalytic converter to burn, as completely as possible, unburned hydrocarbons in vehicle exhausts to reduce emissions even further. Other manufacturers were doing this as well. All this research and development was being done to meet the very stringent emission standards the EPA had set for cars manufactured in the future. Catalytic converters, as most readers know, are canisters about the size of a small muffler with a precious metal matrix, usually platinum, that promotes "post combustion" to further reduce unburned emissions. To put two catalytic converters under a car would have been prohibitively expensive, so manufacturers returned to single exhaust systems. The first such exhaust systems using a catalytic converter were installed on GM cars in 1975, and the dual exhaust was officially history.

Inside Chevrolet, fans of the Z28 lobbied for approval for a dual exhaust system with dual catalytic converters, for that model only—Z28. With its limited production, the additional unique development costs to certify the "dual cat" exhaust system for the Z28, and roughly double the manufacturing cost to put

such a system on the Z28, this proposal was voted down, and with it went the Z28 itself. Some of the engineers and some of Chevrolet's marketing people felt a single exhaust Z28 simply would not sell, and that was the nail in the coffin.

The Camaro line-up for 1975 included the six-cylinder Sport Coupe, the V-8 Sport Coupe, and the Type LT. Prices really started climbing in this year, jumping roughly 20 percent. The price for the six-cylinder Camaro was $3,553.05, the V-8 Camaro was $3,698.05, and the Type LT was $4,070.05. Curiously, in spite of the dramatic price increases and absence of the Z28, sales of the Camaro

The rear spoiler was truly functional and evolved from extensive testing at the GM proving grounds for the second-generation Camaro. This high-profile rear spoiler was available in 1970 as COPO 9796 and could be ordered in place of the standard low-profile design. In 1971 the D80 option included a front spoiler and this taller rear spoiler. The package was standard on the Z28. David Newhardt

In 1973, the solid-lifter LT1 in the Z28 was replaced with the hydraulic-lifter L82. GM switched from a Rochester to a Holley carburetor with a cast-iron (instead of aluminum) intake manifold. In 1974, a new Rochester carburetor fed the L82, and a new Delco-Remy High Energy Ignition (HEI) system replaced the old-style distributor. The finned cast-aluminum valve covers were a distinctive feature of the LT1 and L82 V-8s. Chevrolet

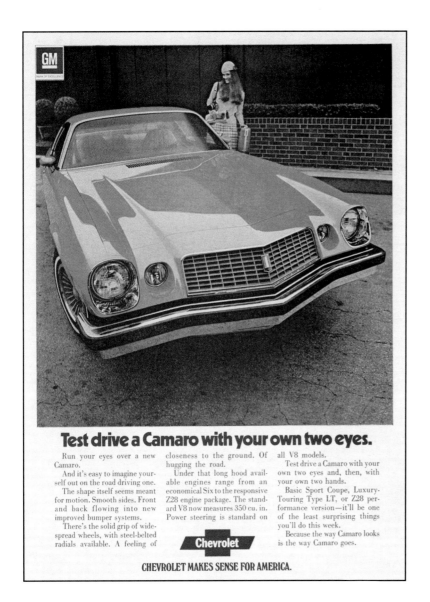

Test drive a Camaro with your own two eyes.

Run your eyes over a new Camaro.

And it's easy to imagine yourself out on the road driving one.

The shape itself seems meant for motion. Smooth sides. Front and back flowing into new improved bumper systems.

There's the solid grip of widespread wheels, with steel-belted radials available. A feeling of closeness to the ground. Of hugging the road.

Under that long hood available engines range from an economical Six to the responsive Z28 engine package. The standard V8 now measures 350 cu. in. Power steering is standard on all V8 models.

Test drive a Camaro with your own two eyes and, then, with your own two hands.

Basic Sport Coupe, Luxury-Touring Type LT, or Z28 performance version—it'll be one of the least surprising things you'll do this week.

Because the way Camaro looks is the way Camaro goes.

Chevrolet

CHEVROLET MAKES SENSE FOR AMERICA.

With Camaro, you can be practical. Or go bananas.

A new look.

Same fine feel.

Front discs standard.

Sport Coupe

Type LT interior.

Deck stripes.

Sport mirrors. *Special Z28 wheels.*

If you can restrain yourself when it comes time to order the extras, you can move into a handsome 1974 Camaro Sport Coupe for less money than you might imagine.

That's one approach. Approach "A" we'll call it.

There's also Approach "Z". The renowned Camaro Z28 package. All the basic good things plus a 350 V8 with 4-barrel, a dual exhaust system, special sport suspension, Positraction rear axle, sport mirrors, F60-15 white-lettered tires and more. If you *really* want to go bananas you can add spoilers and those bold new Z28 hood and deck stripes.

(There's a third approach, comfortably in between: Camaro Type LT with its sumptuous interior and other elegant touches.)

Chevrolet

Camaro. The way it looks is the way it goes.

The redesign of the front and rear of the Camaro in 1974 (to meet bumper low-speed impact standards) was cause for new advertisements to accentuate the fresh, new look of the Camaro. This ad in particular showed how well the bumper was integrated with the redesigned front end.

Chevrolet used this ad to both tout the 1974 Camaro's features and let you know you could have your Camaro mild or wild. It gave brief mention to the Type LT, which would get more ad copy in 1975 with the absence of the Z28.

dropped only slightly from the previous year. Part of the drop could be attributed to the introduction of Chevrolet's new, handsome Monza 2+2, which siphoned off some Camaro buyers. Nearly 30,000 six-cylinder Camaros were sold, and over 116,000 V-8 Camaros rolled off dealers' lots in 1975. Total production was 145,770.

Most significant of the changes on the 1975 Camaro was the larger rear window, which improved visibility. The Camaro now rode on standard radial tires. There were a number of new options, among them power door locks. The Rally Sport option returned for 1975, but it really was little more than a "paint and tape special." The paint scheme of the blacked-out hood and roof contrasting with the body color and matching wheel color was eye-catching, but it did not have a distinctive front end, which made former Rally Sports unique.

The mid-1970s marked a holding pattern for the Camaro. The 1976 models certainly reflected this. There was a new small-block engine, the 305-ci V-8. However, there was much more to this new V-8 than just the loss of 2 cubic inches. The new engine was engineered for the demands of the 1970s and 1980s. This engine had the same 3.48-inch stroke as the 350-ci V-8 coupled with a smaller 3.74-inch bore. Engineers increased intake valve diameter to 1.84 inch and exhaust valve diameter to 1.50 inch. The crankshaft was the same one used in the 350.

There were good reasons Chevrolet didn't simply reintroduce the 307. That engine had been offered in the Camaro from 1969 through the 1973 model year. While the 307 was a good torque engine based on its oversquare design having a bore/stroke ratio of 1.19, it was a poor engine in terms of fuel economy and exhaust emissions. The design of the 305 was driven by the need for a new base V-8 engine that was cleaner and more efficient to operate. The new small-block V-8 had to have a more favorable bore/stroke ratio to satisfy these new requirements. What was done, essentially, was to debore the 350-ci V-8. Joe Bertsch was staff engineer in the V-8 engine group when there was a push to engineer Chevrolet's engines for the best possible emissions and fuel economy.

"The GM Advanced Engineering Group was developing data and theories," says Bertsch, "on the factors affecting the level of unburned hydrocarbons in emissions research in the early 1970s. These factors were the internal surface area of the combustion chamber and the internal crevice volume in the combustion chamber. In the case of the area, the theory was that during combustion, the flame would quench out and incompletely burn in a small boundary layer adjacent to the internal surfaces and be expelled as unburned hydrocarbons during the exhaust stroke. When we got the direction for a 300-ci engine again, instead of reintroducing the 307, which had a 3 7/8-inch bore by a 3 1/4-inch stroke, we decided to retain the crankshaft stroke of the 350 and debore the engine to make it more nearly square."

Denny Davis had joined General Motors in 1949, right out of high school. He graduated from General Motors Institute in 1953 and joined the engine-drafting group as a design draftsman. He moved over to

NEW CAMARO RALLY SPORT.

"Unfair," cried the ordinary cars.

"All's fair in love and cars," retorted Chevrolet, trotting out a knockout new version of Camaro, which was already one of the better looking numbers on the block.

The Camaro Rally Sport is a bright new option package available on either the Sport Coupe or Type LT, in your choice of five colors: red, white, silver, bright yellow or bright blue metallic.

The hood, roof, grille, rocker panels and rear end panels are painted flat black, with distinctive tri-color stripes and Rally Sport I.D.

Rally wheels and dual sport mirrors are included in the package.

Available options (shown) include front and rear spoilers and special 15-inch body-color wheels with white-lettered tires. (The special wheels are available only with the Gymkhana Sport Suspension.)

If you think it looks

good here, wait until you see it in person.

Wait until you walk around it, sit in it, take it on the road.

But don't wait long. Production is limited, and we'd hate for you to miss out.

Now that makes sense
CHEVROLET MAKES SENSE FOR AMERICA.

Chevrolet

Chevrolet brought back the Rally Sport option in 1975 after a 1-year absence. The rear window of the Camaro had been redesigned for greater visibility. The Rally Sport did not feature a different front-end appearance as had been true in the past. Instead, it was a paint and tape special. The spoilers and wheels shown in the ad were separate options.

it on our own—and it just got accepted. As I recall, ultimately it had to go to Don McPherson, who was chief engineer at that time. It was one of those things when someone looked at it and saw it in place, they just didn't argue and made the decision to go with it."

The 1976 Camaros reflected some changes in engine availability. The trusty six-cylinder continued to be an even more popular choice for the frugal. Sales of the six-banger Camaro leapt from 29,749 the previous year to over 38,000 in 1976. The new 140-horsepower 305 V-8 was the standard V-8 in the V-8 Sport Coupe, with a base list price of $3,927.35. In addition, the Type LT no longer came standard with the 350-ci V-8. Instead, the 305 was the standard engine, and the 160-horsepower 350 now became an option. The price for the Type LT jumped nearly 10 percent to $4,320.35. Increased prices didn't affect sales in the least. Total Camaro sales for 1976 were 182,959. To meet the ballooning demand, Chevrolet revived the Van Nuys, California, assembly plant.

F-Body Competition

Pontiac Division and Chevrolet Division in the 1970s were quite autonomous. Nothing proved that more than Chevrolet's decision to stop production of the Z28, and Pontiac's decision to continue building the Firebird Trans Am. Not only did Pontiac forge ahead, it stuffed its monstrous 455-ci V-8s under the hood of the T/A. In 1973, when everyone was down in the face about performance, Pontiac introduced the Super Duty 455 Trans Am, one of the highest performance T/As Pontiac had ever built. It was back again in 1974. With a catalytic converter for 1975 Pontiac dropped the SD455, but still offered a milder 455 in the T/A that year. By 1976, half of all Firebirds sold were Trans Ams. Chevrolet realized it had made a mistake stopping production of the Z28. The division decided to reintroduce the Z28 for 1977.

Chief engineer of the Camaro was now Tom Zimmer. Camaro development engineer was Jack Turner. Jerry Palmer, in charge of Chevrolet's styling, or design studio, would work on giving the revived Z28 a striking new look without expensive tooling costs. Keeping a watchful eye over the new Z28 program was Chevrolet General Manager Bob Lund. There would be no breakthroughs for significant horsepower development, but Zimmer felt much could be done downstream of the catalytic converter to yield

the Corvair engine group in 1957 and two years later landed in Zora Arkus-Duntov's high performance group. Davis rose though the engineering ranks and became basic V-8 engine design group supervisor in 1978. He was closely involved with the 305-ci V-8 program and worked with Joe Bertsch on the program.

"We were told come up with a 5.0-liter engine," Davis says. "I had decided that the thing to do was combine a 3.75-inch bore with a 3.48-inch stoke that gave us something close to 5 liters. We recognized at the time we were talking engines that were felt to be better from an emissions standpoint because of crevice volume, that it should be closer to square— have more stroke and less bore. Joe Bertsch was supervisor of the V-8 group when I was in there. They vacillated so much on this 305 V-8 engine, Joe and I sat down and put together this program and launched a freer-flowing exhaust system. The basically stock 170-horsepower LM1 350-ci V-8 was retained, but a new split exhaust system was developed using dual resonators, which reduced back pressure and gave a very satisfying sound. Zimmer felt better acceleration could be achieved using a high numerical axle ratio, and 3.73:1 was selected as optimum. More important than this, however, was the chassis and suspension development.

Jack Turner decided the original F41 Camaro sport suspension was not adequate for the sophisticated handling parameters he envisioned for the new Z28. The simple, heavy-duty shock absorbers were discarded and shocks with specific valving for better wheel and tire control were engineered. Various front and rear spring rates were evaluated. The front suspension control arm bushings were of a harder compound. Several different front and rear antiroll bar diameters were evaluated until the right balance was achieved; the bushings and grommets isolating the antiroll bars were of a harder durometer, which offered more control. In addition, front and rear spring rates were carefully evaluated to ensure the best combination of ride and handling for any Z28 ever built. All this was done in conjunction with the big GR70-15 tires slated for the car. Countless hours were put in at GM's Milford, Michigan, proving grounds evaluating and refining the suspension under all conceivable, and a few inconceivable, conditions. This included high-speed handling tests at over 100 miles per hour.

Jerry Palmer's studio came up with numerous distinctive touches: front spoiler with integrated wheel well fairings; rear spoiler; blacked-out grille, parking lamp, and headlamp openings; matching body color front and rear bumpers as well as the matching-color stamped steel mag-type wheels; and a nonfunctional NACA-look hood treatment; as well as distinctive interior treatment. It was an eye-catching package. List price would be just under $5,200.

The proof of the Z28, however, was in the driving. Zimmer knew the demanding automotive press would be unforgiving if the new Z did not measure up. The development engineers knew that too. The automotive press would give prospective buyers their first impression of the car. Dealers would not, in all likelihood, have a Z28 to test drive, so magazine test reports had to be positive. All the major automotive

magazines were turned loose on the Z28, and almost without exception, the editors were extremely impressed with the new car. Editor Jim McGraw of *Hot Rod* magazine reflected the consensus among the automotive press when he wrote,

"We're here to tell you that the car is a complete ball to drive . . . unbelievably well balanced, flat and

THE 1975 CAMARO.
IT WON'T DRIVE YOU UP THE WALL.

A car should be a pleasure, not a pain.

And although Camaro, like any car, still requires a certain amount of care and upkeep, we've made some improvements aimed at making it an easier car to live with than before.

Another step closer to the hassle-free car.

Compared to last year, the 1975 Camaro gives you up to 1,500 more miles between recommended oil changes and chassis lubes.

There are no more "points" or ignition condenser to replace, which should simplify tune-ups. And spark plugs, which we used to suggest you change every 6,000 miles or so, should now last up to 22,500 miles.

Fewer pit stops, fewer bucks.

Save hundreds of dollars on upkeep.

With the standard 6-cylinder engine, a 1975 Camaro using unleaded fuel could save you about $300 on tune-ups, oil changes, filters, etc., in 50,000 miles of driving—compared to the 1974 model using leaded fuel—if you follow the Owner's Manual for recommended service. (While parts and labor costs vary throughout the country, we've used current list prices for

parts and a figure of $11 an hour for labor in calculating these savings.)

And as if that weren't enough...

The 1975 Camaro, with High Energy Ignition, is designed to start quicker than before on mornings when it's cold or damp.

And the new Camaro is designed to give off the cleanest exhaust of any Camaro in history, thanks in part to the exclusive use of unleaded fuel.

Drive happily ever after.

Add all that to what Camaro's had going for it right along and we think you'll find it tough to find another car at the price that will please you more —to look at, to drive, to own.

Why not drop by your nearest Chevy dealership for a free test drive and brochure, plus answers to any questions you may have about the new ignition system, the radial tires, the colors, choice of models.

1975 Camaro. The pleasure is all yours.

Now that makes sense.

CHEVROLET MAKES SENSE FOR AMERICA

HOT ROD JULY 1975 **79**

This black-and-white advertisement for the 1975 Camaro appeared in, of all magazines, Hot Rod. *The new theme in advertising was "Chevrolet Makes Sense for America."*

69

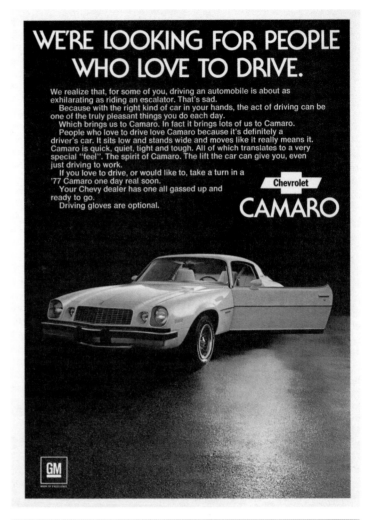

Above: Due to the late introduction of the Z28 for 1977, few ads appeared to announce the car's return. The fine print at the bottom of the ad states: "Turbo HydraMatic required in California." Despite its mid-year introduction, 14,349 Z28s were sold that year.

Above right: This ad for the 1977 Camaro exemplified what had been the basic premise for 20 years. The Camaro wasn't for those who merely saw the car as transportation, but for those who truly loved to drive. The ad copy was directed to as broad an audience as possible

Right: In the late 1970s, the LM1 became the top 350-ci V-8 offered in Camaros, but the flashy aluminum valve covers of the early 1970s were gone. The 1977-1/2 Z28 was rated at 185 horsepower. The 300-plus horsepower of the 1970s LT1 seemed like a distant memory.

almost completely neutral. During off-road 105-mile per hour lane changes . . . the feeling was that every single component in the steering and suspension was united and cohesive in responding to steering inputs. Everything happens right now, and only to the extent of inputs. Steering feel in the wheel and the seat of the pants is excellent, and overall the feeling of this new Z28 is one of lightness and extreme agility. The group of engineers and designers that brought the Z28 out of the ashes stronger than it has been in years is to be congratulated. They have done a terrific job."

Chevrolet was particularly proud of the fact that *Car & Driver's* editors recorded better acceleration times in the 350-ci Z28 than in the 400-ci Pontiac Trans Am. In short, the new Z28 was a worthy successor to previous Zs and an able competitor to the Pontiac Trans Am. Sales of the Camaro for 1977 were 218,853; of these 14,349 were Z28s. It was a very good sales year, and all the better because the Camaro out-sold the Mustang that year. It looked like the Camaro was coming back better than ever. The late 1970s marked the rising fortunes of the second-generation Camaro.

The Chevrolet design studio evaluated several appearance schemes before settling on a monochromatic treatment devoid of chrome trim. The front grille and insides of the headlight bezels and parking lamps were painted flat black. This is another shot of the pre-production prototype. Chevrolet

CHAPTER 4

THE Z28 TRIUMPHANTLY RETURNS

1978 – 1981

With the positive press response to the revived Z28 and encouraging initial sales, Chevrolet General Manager Bob Lund felt bringing the Z back was the right decision. Lund recalled that decision for author Gary Witzenburg in his book, *Camaro! From Challenger to Champion: The Complete History,* published in 1982:

"It was just that we felt we had developed something that was extremely popular at one time in the history of the car, and we had dropped it. Pontiac had come in with their Trans Am and was eating our lunch. We determined that that had to stop. So we resurrected the Z28, which was a household word, so to speak, a byword with the kids. If you had a Z, you were right on top of things. So we brought it back in, and it did help us a lot."

The Camaro underwent a facelift in 1978. The aluminum bumpers were deleted and the Chevrolet studio successfully designed new, flexible urethane front- and rear-end pieces. The new design enhanced the Camaros aesthetic appeal and helped boost sales to a record level—over a quarter of a million were sold. Sales in 1979 were even greater. This 1979 Z28 was one of nearly 85,000 sold that year. David Newhardt

His majesty. The Camaro Z28.

Chevrolet rolled out an aggressive ad campaign promoting the 1978 Z28. The Z28 featured the hoodscoop blister and front fender vents similar to those on the Pontiac Firebird Trans Am. While the Z28 came with a single catalytic converter, Chevrolet engineered a good dual-exhaust system after the converter, offering better performance and a pleasant exhaust note.

The Z28 was a high-profile model that lent real excitement to the whole Camaro line. But Chevrolet was not going to let the Z28 carry all the glory for the Camaro. For 1978, that line would be expanded. There were a total of five distinct Camaro models for that year, all powered by the six-cylinder engine except the Z28. First up was the Camaro Sport Coupe, followed by the Rally Sport Coupe. In the middle of the pack was the Camaro Type LT Coupe. The fourth model was the Camaro Type LT Rally Sport. And at the top of the line was the V-8 Z28.

Inflation was starting to rear its ugly head and the prices of all Camaro models jumped roughly 8 to 10 percent, about $300 to $500. The no-whistles-or-bells six-cylinder Sport Coupe was $4,414.25, while the Z28 listed for $5,603.85. In just three years the price of the Camaro had risen an average of $1,000. Softening the blow was a completely new soft facia front and rear end that gave the aging body design a fresh new look.

On May 11, 1978, the two-millionth Camaro rolled off the assembly line at Van Nuys. (The Norwood, Ohio, assembly plant was also building Camaros, raising the question of why Van Nuys got the honor.) Despite inflationary prices, 1978 proved a record sales year with a total of 272,631 units sold. It was also a sales record for the Camaro flagship, the Z28, with nearly 55,000 sold. Chevrolet could thank the enthusiast magazines for getting the word out just how good the new Z was. *Car & Driver* waxed ecstatic over the Z28, and the magazine's readers valued the editors' opinions.

Since Chevrolet was working on the all-new third-generation Camaro, due for introduction in 1982, there were no stylistic or engineering breakthroughs for the remainder of the second-generation Camaro's production. In 1979 a new model was introduced: the Berlinetta. This was an Italian term most recently attached to Ferraris. The Berlinetta replaced the Type LT, and was basically a different appearance package with more brightwork on the outside. There was a new four-barrel 305, option code LG3, with the rather steep price tag of $235. The engine was rated at 145 horsepower.

In fact, so little of significance was new in the Camaro line that editors were fishing around for what to talk about. All they had to do was look at the window sticker. In the late 1970s a new phrase was

The 1979 Z28 can be distinguished from the 1978 model by the new front airdam and front flairs. Unlike its sister F-body, the Pontiac Trans Am, the 1979 Z28 did not receive the rear wheelwell flairs. David Newhardt

coined: "sticker shock." It hit with full force in 1979. The base six-cylinder Camaro Sport Coupe climbed only $250 roughly, but buyers of the Z28 were slapped with a $500 price increase! Manufacturer's Suggested Retail Price for the 1979 Z28 was now $6,115.35. Was there some new high-output engine to return the Z28 to its glorious days of blistering performance? Nope. In fact, for all practical purposes nothing was changed under the hood of the Z at all.

What was the money going for? In a word: inflation. The automobile is a good gauge on the rate of inflation from year to year. That's because the American automobile is really a product of its countless suppliers as well as the cost of labor to build it. If the prices for supplier parts for the Camaro were going up and the cost of labor to build it also rose, Chevrolet naturally had to pass those costs on to the consumer in order to maintain its profit margin. The price increases in this period would pale in comparison to the price hikes the Camaro would experience in the 1980s.

Despite the sticker shock experienced by Camaro buyers, they signed the purchase agreements willingly and in greater numbers than ever. Sales surpassed the previous year, with 282,571 sold. The biggest selling model was the six-cylinder Sport Coupe, which was scooped up by over 111,000 buyers. The next biggest seller was the Z28, with a

record 84,877 sold. Chevrolet was feeling really good about not only Camaro's sales success, but its entire product line, which also experienced record sales. The good times, however, were about to come to an end.

Recession and Revival

Another gasoline crunch gripped the country at the dawn of a new decade, and once again, supply

The Z28's interior did not change much during the late 1970s. The car came with a 130-mile-per-hour speedometer and tachometer. Z28 drivers wanted to know what was going on under the hood, and the full instrumentation provided the information. David Newhardt

problems caused long lines at the gas pumps. Retail prices for a gallon of regular soared to over $1.50 in some areas and Congress held hearings—with little effect—to determine if there was price gouging going on. In addition to that, America slumped into a deep recession while interest rates zoomed into the double digits. The cost of operating a car and getting a loan was moving people into smaller cars and, in many cases, no new car at all. This recession had a devastating impact on the country. Many small businesses went under and more than a few of them were automobile dealerships. Showroom traffic dropped off to a trickle. There were many critics of President Jimmy Carter's economic policies and he was blamed for much of the country's economic woes. He lost reelection in the Ronald Reagan landslide in November 1979.

Despite all this, Camaro sales for 1979 reached a new record, with over 282,000 sold. Chevrolet was confident it could continue the Camaro's sales success, but it was not to be. As is often the case, recessions often display consumer lag time, and the high interest rates and lack of consumer confidence hit full force in 1980. The Camaro was now in a holding pattern, stylistically. There was virtually nothing to report on the 1980 models in terms of appearance. Under the hood, however, the old straight-six standard engine was finally supplanted by a new 229-ci V-6. There was a new, smaller V-8 displacing 267 cubic inches. It had a bore/stroke ratio of 1.0 and was basically a destroked 305. It offered good fuel economy and a higher level of power than the V-6.

The performance hood blister first appeared on the 1978 Z28, and it was carried over for 1979. The LM1 350-ci V-8 resided under the hood of the 1979 Z28. While not having the punch of the 350s from the early 1970s, the Z28's only contenders on the street were the Trans Am and the Mustang, which were not exempt from the same emissions standards. David Newhardt

Like a trusty soldier, the Z28 returned, but this time the automotive press turned on the very car they had extolled just a couple of years before. The most scathing remarks came from the editors at *Car & Driver,* calling it a "... medieval warrior on the path to a rocking chair ..." and "... a museum piece." Part of the vitriol directed at the Z28 was a result of yet another staggering jump in price. This time the list price for the Z28 jumped over $1,000 to $7,121.32. Inflation was hammering the Z-car with a vengeance. However, there was a new engine under the hood, the 190-horsepower LM1, and this offered a performance improvement over the previous year. Standard on the Z that year was a new functional rear-facing hoodscoop that drew cool, high-pressure hair from the base of the windshield. A solenoid-actuated flap

The tall rear spoiler first appeared in 1970 on the Z28 and received only subtle refinement during the decade. It provided greatly needed downforce at high speeds. David Newhardt

A great deal of engineering and design work went into the front and rear 5-mile-per-hour bumpers with soft urethane plastic fascias that first appeared in 1978. The Camaro's looks were actually enhanced, and the 1979 Berlinetta proved it was a successful effort. Chevrolet

In 1979, Chevrolet introduced the new Berlinetta. This model had a specially engineered suspension, additional insulation surrounding the passenger compartment (to make it quieter), special interior, rocker panel treatment, grille, and Berlinetta nameplates. The Berlinetta was positioned just below the Z28 and above the Rally Sport Coupe in the Camaro line-up that year, replacing the Type LT. Chevrolet

Chevrolet had always referred to the Camaro as "The Hugger" because of its ability to hug curves. In 1979, the Division resorted to tradition and used this in its ad for the Z28. Few prospective Z28 buyers were aware they could also lease it if they wanted, so this ad, which appeared in the February 1979 Hot Rod, *reminded them.*

The basic Camaro Sport Coupe usually did not get much advertising ink, but that changed in 1980 because Chevrolet wanted to promote the new fuel-efficient 3.8-liter V-6, which was standard in the Camaro. The Camaro's numbers were impressive, an EPA-estimated 26 miles per gallon on the highway. Base list price was just under $5,500.

opened upon hard acceleration; during normal driving this remained closed with the engine drawing air through ductwork under the hood.

The 1980 Z28 also had new appearance features. The front fenders now displayed vents; these had been offered on the Pontiac Trans Am for years. Also new were the wheelwell "spats" that had been standard on the Trans Am for 10 years. The Z28 hit a brick wall in terms of sales, plummeting nearly 50 percent. Only 45,137 were sold in 1980; total Camaro sales were a disappointing 152,005. With the recession raging on with no end in sight, and tight gasoline supplies keeping prices high, writers in the automotive press started speculating about the American car as they knew it.

The End of the V-8?

During the later 1970s when the grand experiment known as the "energy crisis" caused long lines at gas stations all across the country, automotive pundits were predicting that the V-8 was doomed. Like dinosaurs facing extinction, it was only a matter of time, some wrote, before the gas-guzzling V-8 would vanish from the face of the earth. Alarmists were wringing their hands saying the world would run out of oil in 50 years. They stated soberly that America had to end its love affair with the automobile. Some automotive journalists were caught up in this crusade and did their best to hammer the nail into the V-8's coffin. Even President Carter made it clear we all had to tighten our belts and make sacrifices.

As many soon found out, there was no immediate shortage of oil, only a shortage of common sense. There was no energy crisis, simply a crisis of confidence. The Arab oil embargo caused many in industry and government to overreact and interfere with the free flow of oil at market prices. When this happened, long lines formed at the pumps, rationing became commonplace, and prices climbed dramatically. The prices were high by U.S. standards, but they were still low compared to what Europeans were used to paying. Americans were clearly spoiled. Cars equipped with big V-8s languished in dealers' showrooms. A few smart buyers snapped up some real bargains certain that gas prices would eventually come down, which they did.

Downsizing became an automotive industry trend. Cars would indeed get smaller, but this kind of

The 3.8-liter V-6 was also standard in the Rally Sport for 1980. This 229-ci engine was available in all states except California. Camaros shipped there received a 231-ci V-6 that had a slightly larger cylinder bore and an automatic transmission. Manual transmissions could not be ordered in California-bound Camaros.

The 1981 Sport Coupe was the last of the second-generation Camaros. It was still a very affordable car with a retail price just under $6,600, and it was the most popular Camaro model that year with over 62,000 sold. Many prospective buyers were eagerly awaiting the release of the third-generation car in 1983.
David Newhardt

The Sport Coupe received the full array of instrumentation instead of non-descript warning lights. The thickly padded steering wheel added to driving comfort. David Newhardt

As a means of boosting performance, Chevrolet worked on developing the Z28's turbocharger. Performance was breathtaking, but the limited number that could be sold coupled with the cost of certification kept the car from production. However, Chevrolet did give the green light to long-time dealer Don Yenko to offer one of his own. The Yenko Turbo-Z went on sale in 1981 and was a very limited production car indeed. Chevrolet

transformation would take several years to accomplish, and it would be at incredible cost. Some enthusiast magazines printed articles saying Camaros of the future would be powered solely by V-6s. Small-block V-8 enthusiasts became anxious. Fortunately, cooler heads prevailed at Chevrolet. The division made the rational decision to offer a mix of V-6 and V-8 engines in the Camaros of the 1980s. Chevrolet said the rumors of the small-block V-8's demise were greatly exaggerated.

The key to the small-block V-8's survival in the 1980s was technology. The two areas where Chevrolet would spend large sums of money for research and development were induction systems and computer controls. These two areas were developed simultaneously and were interlocking. Fuel management, and thus emissions and fuel economy, had to progress by an order of magnitude heretofore unprecedented if Chevrolet was going to meet the standards set by government and the demands of customers. It would be a couple of years before this new technology would become available in the Camaro, but GM was working in earnest to bring it to pass. This technology would also ensure the continuation of the small-block V-8.

That wasn't all. The Camaro body style was indeed aging. In fact, it had been in production for a decade but given new life during that time with striking, new front and rear end styling that helped it to age gracefully. Still, a new Camaro was overdue. In fact, the third generation Camaro was being finalized and prototypes and preproduction units were running around the Milford, Michigan, proving grounds. Security had never been strictly enforced, and General Motors never ran finalized cars around the proving grounds that it did not want the automotive world to see—even through a long telephoto lens. GM knew those plucky freelance photographers were hiding in the bushes outside the security fence perimeter. When the company wanted to "leak" developments to the press, it gave the photographers every opportunity to snap away. All parties understood this, and it certainly did spice up the automotive press when "spy" photos of the forthcoming Camaro first appeared in the November 1980 issue of *Car & Driver*.

The extensive article that appeared in that issue covered the sleek, new Camaro to be introduced for 1982. Editor Rich Ceppos wrote that the new Camaro would be lighter but not much smaller than the current generation car and would offer improvements in engine performance, fuel economy, and most importantly, handling. It was difficult to speculate about the exact configuration of the induction systems being developed for the small-block V-8 for the 1980s, but Ceppos did state improved driveability, fuel economy, and emissions were primary goals. With that, it was hoped, would come improved performance, as well.

For the 1981 Camaro, however, improved performance was not on the menu. All engines were now under the Computer Command Control system to meet the tight 1981 emissions levels. There were casualties in the push to achieve baby's-breath clean exhaust. The Z28 had only an automatic transmission bolted up to the 350 V-8; the four-speed manual transmission could not be ordered on this engine. In addition, output of the engine was lowered to 175 horsepower. To get the thrill of four-on-the-floor, buyers had to opt for the 305 V-8, rated at 165 horsepower with a 3.42:1 axle ratio. Incredibly, with the 350 V-8 in the Z28, the numerical axle ratio was lowered to 3.08:1. This improved fuel economy and emissions but you could forget about acceleration, by whatever definition you chose.

The Rally Sport Camaro was dropped for 1981. There were three basic models that year: the Sport Coupe, the Berlinetta, and the Z28. Prospective buyers in Chevrolet showrooms and on dealers' lots received another round of sticker shock. The base list price for the Sport Coupe was nearly $6,600, the Berlinetta was over $7,300, and the Z28 listed for $8,025.23. The Sport Coupes with standard V-6 were strong sellers with over 52,000 sold to fuel-conscious buyers. However, total Camaro sales continued to decline and by the end of the 1981 model year, only 126,139 Camaros had been sold.

There was room for optimism, however. A new president, Ronald Reagan, had been sworn in that January and the 52 American hostages held by Iran in Teheran since 1979 were finally released. President Reagan survived an assassination attempt by John Hinckley. The economy appeared to be getting back on its feet and it was hoped the new administration would bring inflation under control. For the pony car faithful, however, it was the new Camaro they were all looking forward to.

The 1981 Z28 was the last year for the second-generation, high-performance Camaro. The rear wheel flairs were added on the Z28 in 1980. A total of 43,272 Z28s were sold that year. Paul Johnson/Speed Sports Photography

The Air Induction hoodscoop was functional on the 1980 and 1981 Z28. This 1981 model is finished in Code 51 Bright Yellow. Only 1,816 Camaros were painted this color in 1981. Paul Johnson/Speed Sports Photography

CHAPTER 5

RECREATING THE LEGEND

1982 – 1984

The second-generation Camaro actually had a longer production life than even Chevrolet had anticipated. It's long production life was due to management changes and a battle to determine the next generation's powertrain configuration, and for other reasons. The third-generation Camaro was to be an entirely new car, and this involved considerable design, engineering, and tooling expense. The Camaro had not been selling well at the dawn of the new decade, and Chevrolet had to recapture the excitement and desire the car had once generated. In addition, new and powerful forces would shape Camaro design conceptions.

The 1984 Camaro featured a few suspension improvements that allowed it to beat the Corvette, Ford Mustang SVO, Pontiac Fiero, and Dodge Daytona Turbo Z in Car and Driver's *best-handling American car contest.* Anthony Young

Work on the third-generation F-body cars was begun in the spring of 1975 with a planned introduction for the 1980 model year. With the new Corporate Average Fuel Economy, or CAFE, standards mandated by the government, management was looking at a front-wheel drive configuration for the new Camaro. Cars had to become smaller and lighter to meet those standards. General Motors had years of experience with front-wheel drive, starting with the 1966 Oldsmobile Toronado. Chevrolet had a new, compact front-wheel drive, the Citation, on the drawing board for introduction in 1980. To achieve the CAFE standards, Chevrolet began work on the new Camaro with the assumption that it, too, would be front-wheel drive. The Camaro's powertrain configuration would prove a major battleground even toward the end of the third-generation car's design engineering.

As with all cars, the work began in the design studios. Bill Porter's Advanced No. 1 studio started its work on the F-body layout and configuration, while Jerry Palmer's Chevrolet No. 3 studio focused on establishing the new Camaro's identity in light of its inevitably smaller exterior envelope and proposed

The completely new third-generation Camaro was introduced in 1982 and instantly voted Car of the Year by Motor Trend. *Despite being dramatically downsized (it was 10 inches shorter and nearly 500 pounds lighter), the Camaro was still a substantial-looking car and handsome by anyone's definition. This 1982 Z28 was one of nearly 190,000 Camaros built that year. David Newhardt*

The new dash in the 1982 Camaro was black to reduce glare in the steeply-raked windshield. The instrumentation was strongly influenced by current trends in Italian exoticars. Magazine editors praised Chevrolet for the new Camaro's interior. David Newhardt

front-wheel drive configuration. By March of 1976, scale models had been produced; these models displayed concealed headlights. The new designs also showed shorter doors in response to complaints from both Camaro and Firebird owners that the doors were too long and heavy. To keep the main roof pillar from looking too thick with the shorter door, sliding glass rear windows were added.

The familiar Z28 emblem was found on the dash of the new high-performance Camaro. Chevy's new third generation car made big strides in almost every area. The new interior featured sensibly laid out controls and attractive appointments. David Newhardt

Changing in Midstream

Work progressed on the new Camaro through 1976 and was virtually finalized by March of the following year. Incredibly, however, the decision to go with front- or rear-wheel drive still had not been made. Actually the body had been designed in such a way that either configuration could be used. Introduction of the new Camaro was pushed forward to the 1981 model year. It was around this time that Bill Mitchell, General Motors' dynamic vice president of design, retired. Irv Rybicki stepped into Mitchell's shoes. He wanted to see the progress on the new Camaro. After reviewing the full-size clay buck, Rybicki made it clear he felt the new Camaro should continue the single sideglass theme that had been established with the second-generation car. Aside from that, he liked the new design direction of the third-generation Camaro. Yet his proposed restyling of the door glass was a very significant change and the advanced studio and Palmer's No. 3 studio literally went back to the drawing boards.

With this decision, introduction of the car had to be pushed up again, to 1982. Roger Hughet in Bill Porter's advanced studio did a rendering—of the next-generation Firebird, actually—that served as the basis for a number of clay models. Models were also done of the Camaro. It was quite a striking design. At this stage of design, renderings and models are quite radical, perhaps even impractical. The design invariably becomes more conservative as it takes into

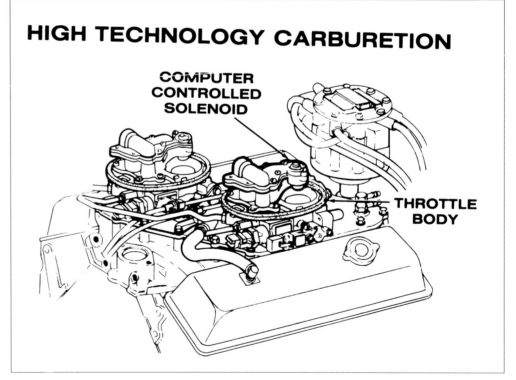

HIGH TECHNOLOGY CARBURETION

COMPUTER CONTROLLED SOLENOID

THROTTLE BODY

GM developed the Throttle Body Injector to surpass the carburetor. Technically, the Throttle Body Injector was not a carburetor, so "High Technology Carburetor" was incorrect. Cross-Fire Injection held the promise of better performance, emissions, and driveability. It succeeded on most counts, but did not perform as well in sub-freezing conditions due to the manifold design. Over 24,000 Z28 buyers in 1982 checked off this option when ordering their cars. This engine was only offered in 1982 and 1983. Chevrolet

account production realities, other costs, and human factors. Nevertheless, it has always been this way in the world of automotive design.

One of the most striking features of this new design was the large glass area—virtually the entire roof structure was to be glass with supporting structure underneath. This influenced the new Camaro design as it evolved, and resulted in the largest and most complex, compound curve rear window ever manufactured when the car went into production.

The powertrain configuration had to be nailed down. Pete Estes, who had overseen the birth of the Camaro as manager of Chevrolet, had been promoted up the corporate ladder and went on to become president of General Motors. He told author Gary Witzenberg the decision regarding the Camaro's powertrain configuration was a very tough call:

"We really had a struggle among ourselves over whether the 1982 was going to be front-drive or rear-drive," Estes said after he had retired from GM. "Finally we decided to make it just as small as we possibly could and stay rear-drive—be able to put a V-8 in it and still have good performance, as well as a four-cylinder engine—tighten it up just as tight as we could, get it as light as possible."

There was also a stylistic battle between Chevrolet and Pontiac over the basics of the F-body design, which the Camaro and Firebird shared. Both GM divisions were pushing for their own distinct look. As before, the cars would share all glass area and roofline, rear quarter panels, and doors. But the entire front end from the firewall forward, and the rear end styling, would be unique. Both divisions had to compromise their stylistic desires somewhat in order to reconcile the portions of the F-body they would have in common.

Just how much smaller was the new Camaro going to be? Overall length was cut 10 inches, and wheelbase was shortened from 108 to 101 inches, making interior packaging a particular challenge. To resolve the interior and trunk requirements, the new Camaro would have a large, practically all-glass hatch. The area behind the rear seats would be open to the hatch; there would be no rear shelf closing off the passenger area from the trunk. The instrument panel designs were strongly influenced by passenger jet cockpit design, with clear legible instruments and controls that were close at hand. The dashboard and instrument panel in the new Camaro would be black regardless of the interior color selected, to minimize reflections from the steeply raked windshield. There was considerable effort invested in designing more ergonomic seats offering lumbar and lateral support along the lines of popular aftermarket seats, and these would have striking fabric graphics and colors.

Under the Sleek New Skin

The goal for the new Camaro was to decrease weight while increasing structural integrity and rigidity. The stub-frame bolted to the partial unit-body on the previous-generation car could not provide this. Computer programs now aided design of a complete unit-body construction; finite element analysis could be performed on the entire structure and individual parts to achieve maximum strength with minimum weight. The actual amount of deflection at any corner of the car could be seen when certain loads were entered into the computer model. Increasing the gauge of the stamped sheet metal component would make it stronger, but also add weight. Computer modeling like this permitted Chevrolet engineers to achieve their goal of dramatically lowering the Camaro's weight while increasing its structural integrity. A more rigid unit-body on the Camaro also contributed to better handling.

The downside of this was greater road noise. The previous design used large synthetic material bushings to isolate the body from the stub-frame. The new-unit body construction required significant development in the area of front control arm bushings and rear spring bushings. To reduce the noise, engineers applied more damping material to key areas of the new Camaro, producing a car that was quieter than the second-generation design.

The same unit-body construction would be used for the four-cylinder Sport Coupe, V-6 Berlinetta, and

The new interior contained distinct, sharp angles. The high-back bucket seats in this 1982 Z28 are cloth and were a definite step-up in comfort compared to the second-generation Camaro interior. David Newhardt

V-8 Z28. Each car would have specific ride and handling parameters, so each car had very specifically engineered spring rates, shock absorbers, and antiroll bars. Even the durometer, or hardness, of the control arm and rear spring bushings was specific to each car.

For the first time, the standard engine in the base Camaro Sport Coupe would be a four-cylinder. This engine, built by Pontiac, displaced 151 cubic inches and was rated at 90 horsepower. The V-6 to go into the Berlinetta displaced 173 cubic inches and was rated at 102 horsepower. Chevrolet chose to drop the 350 V-8 and use the 305-ci small-block, the LG5, with 145 horsepower as the standard V-8 in the Z28. An optional higher performance 305 V-8, engine code LU4, was rated at 165 horsepower. What was really new about these engines was Throttle Body Injection (TBI). The Emission Control System Project Center at the GM Proving Grounds in Milford, Michigan, conducted the research and development of TBI. This group began work in the late 1970s on a new means of low-pressure fuel delivery that was

controlled electronically, but was less complex and less expensive than the Electronic Fuel Injection (EFI) developed earlier.

EFI systems operate using high pressure, between 39 and 79 psi and require an expensive, precise high-pressure fuel pump and an in-tank low-pressure boost pump. GM wanted to develop a low-pressure system that would do away with the expensive, high-pressure pump. It also wanted a specific, programmable electronic control module (ECM) that would monitor all aspects of fuel delivery, emissions, and other aspects during engine operation. ECMs could be specifically engineered for every engine in the General Motors line-up. TBI, with ECM monitoring, achieved smoother operation, better cold and hot starting, better fuel efficiency, and better emissions control. It could even compensate for higher altitudes.

The GM Throttle Body Injection System was introduced on the 1980 Cadillac Eldorado and Seville, in keeping with corporate precedent to introduce the latest technological developments on its premiere car line. Engine development engineer Bill Howell explained the advantages of TBI over regular carburetors:

"Everybody figured throttle body injection wouldn't fly because it was nothing but a force-fed carburetor. When you run it on the dynamometer it doesn't look like anything. When you measure the various parameters, such as mixture distribution and brake-specific fuel consumption, it doesn't look like anything. But, when you put it against the best emissions-controlled carburetor we had in 1979, 1980, and 1981, the car drove worlds better with throttle body fuel injection. It translates to something that's measurable

in car fuel economy and driveability, and the customers love it."

TBI was to be offered on the small-block V-8 in 1982 Camaros and Corvettes. Chevrolet developed a dual TBI performance application and called it Cross-Fire Injection. It featured two TBI units mounted in a staggered position on a new plenum-type intake manifold. In appearance and concept, it harkened back to the days in the late 1960s when the 2x4 barrel carburetor induction system was offered on the Z28—though it by no means developed that kind of power.

Cross Fire Injection—A Disappointment

One of the engineers assigned to TBI development for this system on the Z28 was Louis Cuttitta. He had joined Chevrolet in 1955 and had been totally involved in carburetor and fuel-injection development for more than two decades. This new technology, using two TBIs in developing a performance engine for the Z28 in the 1980s, proved a challenge.

"We got the job of having two of them on the engine," Cuttitta said of the throttle body injectors. "We couldn't have one; we had to have dual TBI for the Corvette and Z28. When we got it, we were told we couldn't change it. Instead, we sent a bunch of boys off to school to learn how this thing works so we could calibrate it—meaning computer chips. We got it to the point where we could get the car to run and meet fuel economy and emissions requirements. But, lo and behold, when we took the car on a trip during cold weather, you would go about 50 feet and it would stall. What we finally found out was the throttle bodies were icing. Ice would form on the throttle bodies to the point it would restrict airflow. You had to open the throttle to the point of being ridiculous and it would stall. This throttle body icing almost killed the concept because these two throttle bodies were located essentially out over the valve covers. There was no way to get any exhaust heat up there, as you could with a carburetor.

"Remember the original Z28 Camaro that Penske raced? It had two Holley four-barrels on it. The one where the carburetors sat out over the valve covers. *That* inlet manifold was what we got stuck with for the TBI! The throttle bodies were just adapted to that manifold, because they already had the dies and the money spent."

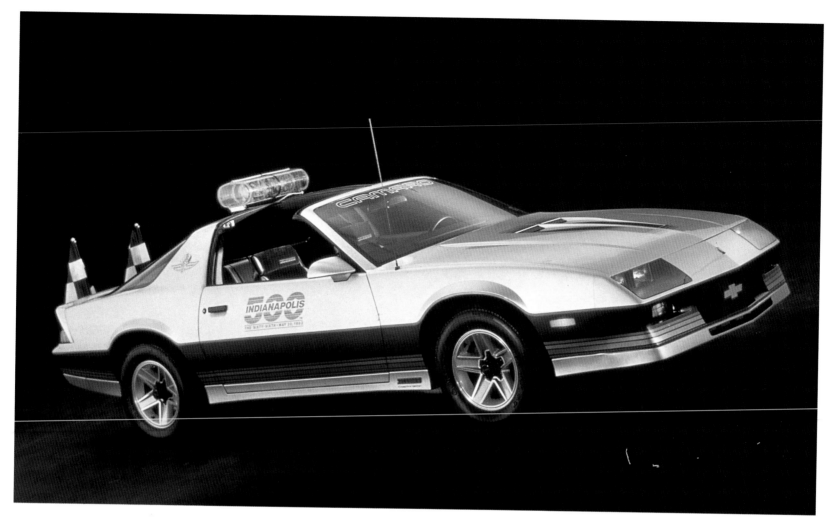

Cuttitta and his team developed a means of getting hot air to the air cleaner, and the warm air prevented the TBI units from icing up during cold weather operation. But there was another problem with Cross Fire Injection that surfaced during pilot testing of the Z28 prior to production. It was known among Chevrolet engineers as the infamous "Robo Car Wash Incident." When this car, with fresh air hood, went through a Robo Car Wash, the high-pressure water jets forced open the flaps in the fresh air hood and water poured into the Cross Fire Injection air cleaner—literally flooding the engine. Chevrolet engineers tried various quick fixes, but there was not enough time to redesign the hood intake to solve the problem. Aside from that, Chevrolet was still struggling with emissions and CAFE standards, while at the same time trying to extract an acceptable level of performance for the Z28. It proved to be an elusive goal.

The New Camaro is Introduced

The new Camaro was eagerly awaited by the automotive press, and expectations were high. It had been a long wait. As usual, introduction of the new Camaro was delayed several months, but all the automotive magazines had cover stories for their January 1982 issues. Almost to an editor, they extolled the new Camaro's handling as the best of any Camaro ever built, and ranked the Z28 as among the best-handling cars in the world. Steering response was extremely quick. Braking with the new, fatter tires hauled the car down from 60 miles per hour in only 157 feet. Despite being 10 inches shorter and several inches narrower, the lines of the Camaro were so well executed it gave no indication of being downsized. And the car was undeniably handsome. *Motor Trend* stated, "Besides being good looking, it just may be the best-handling car built in America."

The 1982 Z28 was selected to pace the 66th running of the Indianapolis 500. The pace cars featured an all-aluminum small-block 350-ci V-8 with considerably more power than the V-8 offered in the production Z28. The Z28's suspension needed virtually no enhancements to handle its duties at the legendary oval track. Chevrolet

Chevrolet offered a pace car replica to commemorate the selection of the Z28 to pace the 66th running of the Indianapolis 500 and displayed the Indy Pace Car replica at the International Automobile Show in Detroit in January 1982. The pace car replica offered for sale had the RPO Z50 and a total of 6,360 were sold. The new, third-generation Camaro received top billing at the show with the large display overhead reading, "CAMARO . . . Its closest competition is its own shadow."

And what of performance? In the Z28 equipped with the Cross-Fire Injection 305 V-8, all the editors could state with honesty was, "Power is sufficient to keep you abreast of RX-7s and 924s." Note the editors didn't say *out accelerate* RX-7s and 924s. Part of the problem was the unavailability of a four-speed manual transmission with the Cross-Fire Injection 305; only a three-speed automatic with 3.23:1 rear axle was offered. And this was an expensive option in the Z28 at $450. With the standard four-barrel 305 V-8 rated at 145 horsepower, you could order up the four-speed. Price for the new Camaro Z28 leapt to over $10,000. That didn't deter nearly 65,000 eager drivers from buying one, even if it did take nearly 10 seconds to get to 60 miles per hour. The 1982 Z28 took 17.13 seconds to cover the quarter-mile, making it the slowest Z Chevrolet had ever built.

Nevertheless, *Motor Trend* Voted the 1982 Camaro Z28 "Car of the Year."

The editors at *Car & Driver* were less conciliatory. Yes, the new Camaro went on a weight loss program, but not enough to make up for the loss in horsepower. The editors argued that with the Camaro's stunning good looks and superb handling, the stiff price tag should ensure brisk performance, but it just wasn't there. The fact was the new Camaro program, like every automotive program, had a budget. The financial pie had to be carved up accordingly, and the smallest piece of the pie was given to engine development. Certainly Chevrolet engineers were aware of this during the program and knew there would be squawks when the Z28 was tested.

"The fastest Camaro money can buy," *Car & Driver* wrote, "runs with a crude three-speed Turbo

1983 CHEVROLET CAMARO

The Z28 was prominently displayed on the cover of the 1983 Camaro brochure. The performance hood on the 1982 and 1983 Z28 was fiberglass, not stamped steel. In 1984 Chevrolet switched to steel stampings.

HydraMatic, a lame 5,000-rpm redline, a measly 165 horsepower, and a compromising 3.23:1 axle ratio. This is not the stuff of dreams, particularly when it's saddled with 1.7 tons of mass. Zero to 60 takes 7.9 seconds; a quarter-mile and 85 miles per hour come up in 16.0 seconds. High-output Mustangs and Capris are long gone."

As if to drive home that point, *Road & Track* conducted a side-by-side road test of the 1982 Z28 and Mustang GT 5.0. The Mustang GT recorded a 0–60 time of 8.0 seconds to the Z28's 9.7 seconds. In fact, any zero to whatever speed left the Z28 looking at the Mustang GT's taillights. The editors did rate the Mustang GT a poor second in the handling department, and in steering. In the end, the editors felt there was no clear-cut winner. They did lament the Z28's disappointing power, however.

The performance engine development dollars would have to wait until after the third-generation Camaro was out the door. But not all Camaro buyers were looking at the Z28. In fact, as had always been the case, sales of the Z28 were only a fraction of total Camaro sales. The four-cylinder Sport Coupe and the V-6 Berlinetta were good sellers. The Sport Coupe was very popular with buyers in 1982, with 78,761 sold. Nearly 40,000 Berlinettas were sold that year.

Performance Begins to Return

Although buyers had yet to see it, Chevrolet had been doing performance development work on the 305. The Camaro would have new and improved offerings for 1983, with new transmissions as well. The Cross-Fire Injection LU5's output was upped to 175 horsepower. The standard 305 in the Z28 was rated at 150 horsepower. A new standard five-speed manual transmission gave better gear ratios for acceleration with the bonus of improved highway mileage when in fifth gear. There was a new automatic overdrive transmission, a product, really, of the CAFE standards GM was forced to meet. It was very expensive at $525, but nearly 69,000 buyers chose this powertrain. The five-speed manual was only $125 and over 32,000 Camaro buyers opted for this transmission. The three-speed automatic transmission cost $425 and was installed in nearly 50,000 Camaros. The big news in performance came in the spring of 1983—April to be exact.

The limitations of Cross-Fire Injection became evident during development testing in the engine labs and out at Milford Proving Grounds. The Advance Engine Group was put to work on a higher output 305 using a traditional four-barrel carburetor. Rochester carburetor was tasked to develop a carburetor to suit this package. A compression ratio of 9.5:1 was selected and camshafts were tested until one was found to deliver power as well as low emissions. To get additional horsepower the intake and exhaust systems were modified. A dual-snorkel air cleaner improved air intake, and larger diameter exhaust and tailpipes, behind a wide-mouth, lower-restriction catalytic converter from the Corvette, gave freer exhaust. The High Output 5.0 V-8 developed 190 horsepower at 4,800 rpm with 240 ft-lb of torque at 3,200 rpm. This engine had a somewhat controversial option code.

"When we went to what would ultimately be the Camaro high-performance package," says engineer Denny Davis, who worked on this engine, "I was told to go back and get one of the old high-performance RPO numbers that were no longer used and put it on the 305 four-barrel package. Well, GM in its infinite wisdom, reused those old RPO numbers for something else after they went out of production. So all the old high-performance numbers that we had back in the 1960s had been assigned to other packages. So I said, 'OK guys, if you can't give me any of those, give me a new RPO to go with this engine.' So they came up with some lousy number, and I called them up and said, 'Guys, this stinks. This has got no pizzazz at all. After all the other Z packages and everything we've had, I want something with sex appeal. Get me something other than

this thing.' We had L engine designations whether we wanted them or not. So they called me back and said it would be L69. They thought I would holler. I just laughed and said, 'I love it guys. I'm going to leave it.'"

The L69 was a dramatic improvement over the Cross-Fire Injection 305. Coupled to the five-speed manual transmission, a Z28 could now reach 60 miles per hour in just over seven seconds. The option price of the L69 was $450. Because it was introduced so late in the 1983 model year, only 3,223 were ordered in Z28s that year. Prices for the Sport Coupe, Berlinetta, and Z28 had finally leveled off; in fact, the price of the Z28 dropped over $500 to $10,336. Yet sales of the Camaro declined in 1983, to 154,381 sold.

The Berlinetta Goes High Tech

Chevrolet decided that it would make its mid-model, the Berlinetta, more distinctive for 1984. The date had a symbolism of its own as the title of George Orwell's dark and futuristic novel, which sold hundreds of thousands of copies that year. Chevrolet had no dark plans, but it did move to introduce high technology to the Berlinetta. That year the model received a completely new instrument and console design.

The Chevrolet Interior Studio had been hard at work to move the Camaro from the analog 1970s to the digital 1980s. The 1984 Berlinetta interior was the result. Virtually every conceivable vehicle function, and a few inconceivable functions, were mounted in two pods on each side of the steering column. The radio/cassette player was mounted on a separate pod, angled toward the driver and all these pods were designed to be within easy reach. There was heavy emphasis on graphic symbols instead of words—very European, you see. The speedometer was a large digital readout, and the tachometer to the right operated like a digital graphic equalizer, with lighted bars that climbed with the rpms. Within this area were analog gauges for fuel, water temperature, and electrical system voltage, and various warning lights. But wait—that's not all! There was also an overhead console, which gave elapsed mileage in kilometers and miles, and featured map light, detachable penlight, and even a cigarette pouch.

The third-generation Camaro had a drag coefficient of 0.34. This was crucial to improve GM's CAFE (Corporate Average Fuel Economy) standards. More than 78,000 buyer chose the four-cylinder Sport Coupe in 1982, but nearly 65,000 bought the Z28. This 1984 model was among the more than 100,000 Z28s sold that year. **Anthony Young**

Chevrolet decided against offering a Camaro convertible for the third generation; only the hardtop was available. The rear window was one of the largest pieces of automotive glass ever made and was a marvel of engineering. Anthony Young

The hallmark of every Camaro is its enduring and undated styling. This 1984 Z28 has remained in the hands of its original owners since it was new. It is one of nearly 52,457 Z28s ordered with the L69 four-barrel 305-ci V-8. Anthony Young

The editors of *Car & Driver* tested a 1984 Berlinetta with optional four-barrel 305, removable glass roof panels and numerous other options, which pushed the price up to nearly $14,000. What did the editors think of the instrumentation that looked like it was lifted from Han Solo's *Millennium Falcon*?

"Pinball wizards, unite!" they wrote. "Bells, whistles, control pods everywhere! Buttons for this, buttons for that, tabs and sliders for everything else. Zillions of little controlettes, everyone of them matte black and every one of them intended to be different and to work in new ways. And to think that years passed before Detroit realized that maybe there really was something to the idea of putting dimmer switches on steering-column stalks."

However valiant the effort by Chevrolet, the editors felt it was technology for the sake of the "gee whiz" factor, and not human factors. Many of the control buttons in the two pods were obscured by the steering wheel, and the radio/cassette pod vibrated alarmingly over bumpy roads. The three road test editors gave this effort a thumbs down, but overall liked the Berlinetta very much. Buyers, at any rate, were dazzled with the car and sales of the Berlinetta

The L69 became an available option in 1983. It was formally identified as H.O. 5.0-liter V-8. It came with a Rochester Quadrajet four-barrel carburetor, radical cam timing, and a healthy 190 horsepower at 4,800 rpm. It could accelerate to 60 miles per hour in 7.2 seconds. Anthony Young

climbed to 33,400 for 1984. In fact, overall sales of the Camaro did an about-face that year. Interest rates were down and sales totaled 261,591.

The L69 (cries of "Four-barrels rule!" were often heard that year) was the hot ticket to boost the Z28's performance and the Cross-Fire Injection 305 was dropped. An impressive 52,457 buyers checked the L69 option box. There were no significant changes or additions to the Z28, and they weren't necessary. The magazine awards started rolling in.

Road & Track selected the Camaro as one of the 12 best cars in the world. *Car & Driver* selected the 1984 Z28 as the best-handling car built in America. The Chevrolet engineers behind the third-generation Z28 were all smiles.

And Chevrolet Division was smiling too. Its answer to the Mustang was doing extremely well as the middle of the decade approached. Executives were also smiling because they knew what was going to enter Chevrolet showrooms in the years to come. Performance was about to return to the Camaro in a very big way.

Z28s ordered with the L69 received this identification on the left rear bumper. Similar identification appeared on the rocker panels. Anthony Young

HIGH-PERFORMANCE RENAISSANCE

1 9 8 5 — 1 9 8 8

The 1985 model year was the Camaro's fourth year of production in its third-generation evolution. The car was about to enter a new and exciting phase of development, in which the third generation was improved and refined. The research and development dollars had finally been freed to enhance V-8 performance and create even better handling capability. Chevrolet engineering was painfully aware of the performance shortcomings of the small-block V-8. As good as the four-barrel L69 was in the Z28, the future of Chevrolet's venerable V-8 was pointing to fuel injection, not a four-barrel carburetor or even Throttle Body Injection.

Tuned Port Injection

In 1982, Denny Davis was promoted from his position as supervisor of the basic engine group to the newly formed advanced engine design group. A

After a nearly 20-year absence, the Camaro convertible returned in 1987. Automobile Speciality Company performed this special—and expensive—conversion for Chevrolet. The convertible was available on the base Camaro and the Z28. Only 263 Sport Coupe Convertibles and 744 Z28 convertibles were built in 1987. Chevrolet

The IROC Sport Equipment Package stuffed the widest aluminum wheels and fattest tires into the wheelwells of the Z28. The car rode on 16x8-inch cast-aluminum wheels and were mounted with Goodyear Eagle P245/50VR tires. With the suspension and chassis modifications as part of the package, the IROC-Z was capable of .92 g lateral acceleration. David Newhardt

Many styling cues from the second-generation Camaro, such as the taillight detail, were carried over to the third-generation car to maintain stylistic continuity. The rear spoiler was less pronounced, but still functional. David Newhardt

radically new induction system for the small-block V-8 started to take shape in the basic engine group under the direction of Frank Langenstein. It all came about with a decision to make the 305-ci V-8 the largest displacement V-8 available in the Camaro and Corvette in the future. Davis recalled the story:

"Because of constraints on fuel economy, we would get edicts: 'You are not going to have engines larger than 305 cubic inches.' That's really how the 305 high-performance stuff got developed. It was going to be *the* engine size—including the Corvette. The fuel injection package was developed for the 305. I tried to develop the fuel injection package for a 350 and was told, 'Keep this up and you're going to be fired. It's going to be sized for the 305-ci engine. That's the biggest engine it's ever going on. You're not going to get the 350-ci engine, so don't worry about it.'

"And I said, 'I don't believe you guys, because this happens at the 11th hour all the time.'

"So, we developed the 305 along those auspices and, of course, guess what happened? Along

came the Corvette. They said, 'We want that performance. We don't want to lose our image. We want the most potent machine we can get. We can handle 350 cubic inches. Put it on the 350.' So it was sized for the 305 and incorporated on the 350 after the fact. That was the reason the 305 got any high-performance development at all. I was pushing to do it, but I was constrained considerably."

Bob Wiltse concurs with this interpretation of events. Having spent many years with Chevrolet, Wiltse finally became chief engineer of the Engine Control Technology Center in the late 1980s and contributed to the development of Tuned Port Injection (TPI). When asked what was the impetus for developing Tuned Port Injection, Wiltse responded:

"Horsepower for the Corvette. What our original assignment was from a fuel economy standpoint was to tune the torque peak on the 5.0-liter V-8 to produce the same torque as a 5.7-liter V-8 with TBI (Throttle Body Injection). So we put ram-tuned runners on the 5.0-liter and as we started to develop that technology, we found we could get the improved fuel economy out of the 5.7-liter."

An induction system as sophisticated and cutting-edge as Tuned Port Injection has many people working on it. It was important to have engineers with vast experience to draw upon in the various aspects of design and development. One of them was Jim Walker, who cut his engineering teeth on

the Vega engine program starting in 1968. He formally transferred to Chevrolet in 1970.

"My first involvement with the small-block was as assistant staff engineer for base engine," said Walker in 1991. "Base engine is defined as the engine as it is shipped from the plant, which includes heads, block, intake manifold, exhaust manifolds, and oil pan, but before it gets the accessory drives and fuel injection and engine controls. Tuned Port allowed us

An IROC-Z medallion was mounted to the dashboard on the passenger side. David Newhardt

The rocker panel Z28 identification included the engine displacement. For 1987, 12,105 IROC-Zs were fitted with the 5.7-liter (350-ci) Tuned Port Injection V-8. David Newhardt

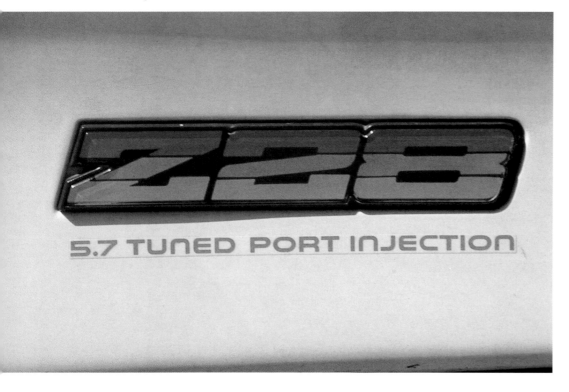

to tune the intake and exhaust for better airflow through the engine for more power. Port fuel injection allows fuel to each individual cylinder, computer controlled, for more precise fueling for better emission control and improved performance.

"The design and fabrication of the intake manifold came under the base engine group," Walker said. "Also, a lot of thought went into the design relative to the appearance. It's not a cheap system from a manufacturing standpoint, but we wanted the air flow, and we wanted a tuned port fuel injection system for the power, economy, and emissions, and the aesthetics so it looked like a powerful engine."

"The one thing about Tuned Port Injection," said Louis Cuttitta, "was it started with a clean sheet of paper. You had enough room in the engine compartment to do that. The development engineers and the design engineers were given a free hand. The Number One goal was to get horsepower. That's why there was impetus to put all this money into one basket. However, the car still had to cold start, idle, and had to be able to run in city traffic with no hiccups. That's why the money was spent and the development done. It wasn't done by a few people, it was done by a great many laboratory and engineering staff people, and it was done well."

The exotic-looking Tuned Port Injection was introduced as an option in the 1985 Camaro Z28. With the RPO engine code LB9, it was the top optional engine available that year, costing nearly $700. This 305-ci V-8 with TPI was rated at 215 horsepower at 4,400 rpm with 275 ft-lb of torque at 3,200 rpm. It had been an entire decade since the small-block V-8 had been rated over 200 horsepower in the Z28.

The IROC Legend

In 1973 a new racing series was launched in the United States, the International Race of Champions, or IROC, for short. The goal was to have 12 professional race drivers from diverse backgrounds compete in identically equipped cars—and may the best man win. These drivers were champions in their respective racing field of expertise: stock car, grand prix, etc. The cars and drivers would compete on both road courses and oval tracks. It was quite a clever concept, actually. The first year used Porsche RSRs, but then Chevrolet did an amazing thing. It succeeded in convincing IROC management to race Camaros. They would be much less expensive to build, Chevrolet argued, and they would be *American*. This made sense to the IROC folks, and Chevrolet was off and running, and gaining much needed division prestige. (See chapter 10 for the full IROC story.) It would be 10 years, however, before Chevrolet would build a namesake Camaro celebrating its long involvement in the IROC series.

For 1985, Chevrolet introduced the Camaro IROC-Z. Chevrolet engineers had indeed been working on moving the Z28 even further in its handling capability. This was driven in part by tire technology, where the aspect ratio—the ratio of width to height—was increasing dramatically. The IROC-Z development program stipulated a shift from 15-inch wheels to 16-inch wheels with Goodyear 245.50VR16 "Gatorback" tires. The ride height of the car was lowered 15 milimeters, lowering the center of gravity. The Delco front struts were engineered with different valving, with Bilstein gas-charged shocks in the rear for better ride control. The front wheel caster was increased from 3 to 4 degrees. During the vigorous suspension testing, engineers discovered the front frame rails were deflecting due to the high cornering loads placed on the chassis, so a tubular brace was designed to tie the frame rails together, mounted beneath the steering gear near the front antiroll bar. The diameter of the rear antiroll bar was increased from 1 to 24 milimeters. Even the hydraulic steering system was revised to provide less assist and give more feel of handling inputs.

The IROC Sporting Equipment Package with the option code B4Z could be ordered on the Z28 for $659. When coupled with either the L69 four-barrel 305 with five-speed manual transmission, or the LB9 Tuned Port Injection 305 with overdrive automatic transmission, the resulting IROC-Z became one of the best all-around performance cars in the world. This car could generate .84 to .89 lateral Gs on the skid pad, but that was merely steady state cornering. Handling capability of this new Camaro was an order of magnitude above what had come before.

Motor Trend had glowing praise for the car: "This is serious cornering power, of a magnitude previously reserved for hard-core sports cars, and indicative of how far technology has taken us. The IROC-Z is a responsive, precise, hard-cornering weapon that will humble many Euro/Japanese cars sporting much fancier window stickers. The 0–30 mile per hour acceleration time (2.24 seconds) is among the fastest

The cover of the oversized 1987 Camaro brochure prominently featured a bold close-up image of the IROC-Z. Despite the Camaro's stunning looks and stirring performance, sales in 1987 were less than half that of 1979 when a record 282,571 were sold. Price was inversely proportional to sales; the base list price of the 1987 Z28 had more than doubled since 1979.

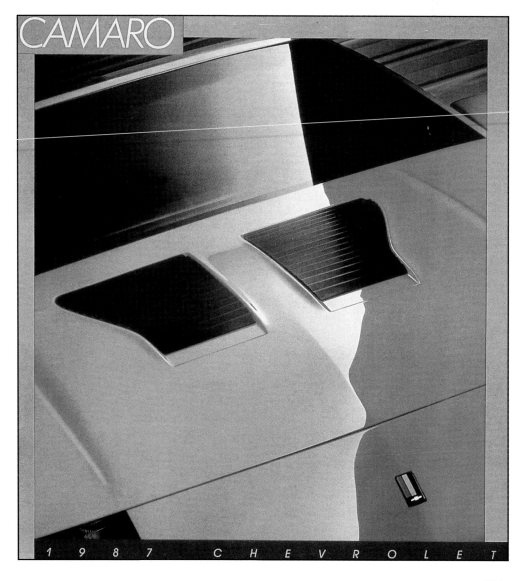

Tuned Port Injection (TPI) was first offered on the 305-ci small-block V-8 in 1985. The RPO code was LB9. In 1987, Chevrolet brought back the 350-ci V-8, which had been unavailable in the Z28 after 1981. This new 350 was also fitted with Tuned Port Injection and had the RPO code B2L. Chevrolet used 5.0 and 5.7 (for liters) designations to announce displacement instead of cubic inches. Chevrolet

of all the cars we've tested at MT, in such exalted company as Porsche Carrera (2.06), Lotus Esprit Turbo (2.02), and Chevrolet Corvette (2.22)."

The ever-hard-to-please editors at *Car & Driver* drove both an L69 and a LB9 TPI IROC-Z for its October 1984 preview issue. They wrote: "Gone are all traces of crudeness. The IROC-Z's way with the road is now admirably supple and smooth. It keeps all four paws firmly planted, even over bombed-out pavement—and it does so with impressive ease. The steering is delightfully accurate, and the fat tires seem to stick as if they had been dipped in glue. No doubt about it, you can make graceful moves in this car now; no matter how hard you push, it doesn't get ruffled. Even the Lear driver's seat finally feels right. And does it ever go. The L69-and-five-speed combination blasts to 60 miles per hour in 7.5 seconds and doesn't quit until it's hit 138 miles per hour. Without a doubt, the IROC-Z is the best all-around Camaro ever."

The IROC-Z's appearance was distinguished by the addition of driving lights in the center grille area, a performance hood with nonfunctional louvers, matching color lower beltline (as opposed to the Z28 color contrasting lower beltline), and bold IROC-Z graphics on the doors.

For the first time, the price of the base Camaro Sport Coupe broke through the $8,000 barrier—and that was with a four-cylinder engine! Just four years before, that price was what you paid for a Z28. Both the six-cylinder Berlinetta and the V-8 Z28 had an identical MSRP of $11,060. Still, the Z28 with the IROC-Z option made it one of the best all-around performance cars in the world, able to hold its own with some of the most expensive performance cars from England and Europe at a fraction of the cost.

And how did the Camaro fare against its life-long nemesis, the Mustang? *Motor Trend* put the L69 IROC-Z up against the turbocharged SVO Mustang in its July 1985 issue. They took the two cars to a nearby racetrack (they didn't state which one) and put the cars through their paces—the cars were, after all, no longer just straight-line machines. Although the IROC-Z showed better acceleration times, the two competitors were within half a second of each other around the track, with the Camaro lapping the course in 1.27.42 and the Mustang a few tenths faster at 1.26.73—a virtual dead heat.

Despite the dramatic improvements made to the Z28 in the form of the IROC-Z and other areas of the Camaro, sales for 1985 plunged dramatically compared to the record sales year in 1984, dropping to 180,018 cars from 261,591. These wildly fluctuating sales figures were as much a result of equally fluctuating interest rates and the capricious insurance rates as anything else.

Mid-decade Refinement

By the mid-1980s, America and the world had seen some momentous events, and 1985 had proved no exception. Ronald Reagan had been sworn in for a second term as president, Soviet Premier Chernenko died and former KGB head Mikhail Gorbachev took over; the Walker family spy ring was caught and tried for doing untold damage to American national security; the Italian cruise ship *Achille Lauro* was seized by terrorists; and the fourth space shuttle, *Atlantis,* made its maiden launch on October 3.

The 1986 Camaro models marked another plateau year, with no changes aesthetically and few mechanically. The old, reliable four-speed manual transmission was finally dropped from the powertrain line-up, superseded by the more refined and sophisticated five-speed that had been in production

for several years. The base Sport Coupe benefited from an upgraded sport suspension, better wheels and tires, standard power steering and brakes, an improved exhaust system, AM radio, and other aesthetic changes. These refinements pushed the base list price to $9,349. Despite this, the Sport Coupe remained the most popular Camaro model with almost 100,000 sold in 1986. Production of the Berlinetta continued for only a few months before Chevrolet halted production. Sales had been declining for several years and it was at the bottom of Camaro sales. The Z28 and IROC-Z options returned virtually unchanged.

The June 1986 issue of *Automobile* magazine contained a very interesting road test. Editor Dean Batchelor was handed a pilot production IROC-Z fitted with the TPI 350-ci L98, as installed in the Corvette. Acceleration times were impressive, with the car reaching 60 miles per hour in 6.2 seconds and covering the quarter-mile in 14.5 seconds with the four-speed automatic. Handling was "IROC Awesome," as expected. Besides the $995 tab for the 350 V-8, there were four mandatory options. These options included Posi-Traction rear axle ($100), oil cooler ($110), four-wheel disc brakes ($179), and four-speed automatic transmission ($465). In addition, Chevrolet deleted two options—air conditioning, due to lack of space for a larger radiator to handle greater cooling demands, and the T-top, with its removable roof sections. This was definitely a northern climate car only.

When crazed motorheads walked into Chevrolet showrooms waving the June issue of *Automobile* and asked how they could order one, they were greeted with baffled expressions from the salesmen. They knew nothing about it. Calls to other dealers and regional managers proved vague. Calls to Chevrolet's Central Office finally produced the statement that the car had not actually gone into production yet. The summer months dragged on and still no one could order one. It is rumored that certification of the L98 IROC-Z was finally approved and a small number built in the 1986 model year, but it would really be 1987 before the car officially entered production. The end-of-year production total for 1986 was up slightly from the previous year, with 192,219 Camaros sold. There were rumors, too, that spy photographers had spotted *convertible* Camaros at the GM Proving Grounds in Michigan.

The Camaro left its plateau in 1987 and took flight. The 350-ci high-performance V-8, option code B2L, officially was offered as an option in the IROC-Z, listing for $1,045. Unlike the 350 in the Corvette, this engine in the IROC-Z came with iron instead of aluminum cylinder heads and an iron exhaust manifold instead of the Corvette's stainless steel tube setup. Rated at 225 horsepower, it was only available with the four-speed automatic transmission. However, the auto transmission was so good and the shift points so precise, it was a perfect match for the torquey 350, and the car recorded excellent acceleration times.

The other big news was the return of the convertible to the Camaro line. These new ragtops were not built by Chevrolet, but were hardtop conversions performed by ASC. This company, originally with the name American Sunroof Corporation, made and installed the T-tops for GM in the 1970s. Eventually, GM took over the manufacture and installation of T-tops in its cars and ASC expanded into convertible conversions. To reflect this move, the company created a division called the Automobile Specialty Company. Within this division was the Limited Edition Vehicles Group, which performed the conversion to the Camaro Sport Coupe and Z28. The price of the conversion was breathtaking—nearly $5,000. List price for the 1987 Camaro Sport Coupe was $10,409 and the convertible was $15,208. The Z28 was listed at $13,233 and the Z28 convertible listed at $17,632.

The cars delivered to ASC for conversion came with factory-installed T-tops because these cars had additional unibody reinforcement to reduce body flex. The convertible conversion required additional structural reinforcement in the rocker panels, floorpan, the cowl, and rear quarter panels. Despite the expense, the top was not electrically powered, but manually operated. Those wanting the wind in their hair and sun in their face did not care—this was the first Camaro convertible since 1969! The conversion added about 150 pounds to the car's weight. ASC had the capability of building 60 Camaro convertibles

The TPI 5.0-liter (305-ci) LB9 V-8 option was much more popular than the 5.7-liter (350-ci) B2L in the 1987 IROC-Z. This 1987 model owned by Adam Billing was one of 28,370 ordered with the LB9 V-8. Anthony Young

a week. The cars were sold only through selected Chevrolet dealers, because not every dealer was capable of performing the warranty work on the car if it ever needed it.

The Camaro convertible, whether Sport Coupe or Z28, was a very limited commodity, and the laws of supply and demand became immediately apparent. Suggested list price usually went out the window, with dealers adding on what they felt the market would handle. Some dealers in Miami, Florida, tacked on a surcharge that pushed the convertible option up to $8,800—and the cars sold. As more cars became available and demand slowed, the price also came down, but ever so slowly. But those with nearly $25,000 burning a hole in their pocket for a ragtop IROC-Z didn't care. The 350 V-8, unfortunately, could not be ordered in the IROC-Z convertible.

Many prospective Camaro convertible buyers were unaware of its availability because of its midyear offering. Some were put off by the high price. Only 263 Sport Coupe Convertibles with standard V-8, and 744 Z28 convertibles were ordered for 1987.

There was another Camaro added to the line that was actually conceived at the Van Nuys, California, assembly plant. Chevrolet's West Coast marketing manager at the time, John Burrow, was challenged by Chevrolet Division to take the pulse of California and have the factory come up with a very sporty yet fuel-efficient Camaro that would appeal to buyers in that huge state. The plant manager was pulled in and was all smiles when he learned of the plan. He, in turn, called in the key Camaro production people and told them the idea. The plant came alive. Working with Hank Haga at GM Design's Advanced Concept Center, the group devised a Camaro with the Z28's ground effects and spoilers, wheels and tires and interior, cloaked in a monochrome paint scheme—no big decals or contrasting color schemes—and powered by the 2.8-liter (173-ci) V-6. The insurance tariff on a Z28 was pretty steep in any part of the country, but this car was designed to get around it and be more fuel efficient to boot. The price was not much less than a Z28, however—just under $13,000. It was, on the other hand, very insurance friendly. The car was dubbed the Camaro RS.

The Camaro had become quite a refined automobile by the late 1980s and more than capable of

The choice between the five-speed manual or the four-speed automatic transmission was one reason for the popularity of the LB9 TPI 5.0-liter V-8. The B2L (350-ci V-8) was only available with automatic transmission. Billing's 1987 IROC-Z is finished in Code 68 Dark Brown Metallic. Only 1,633 Camaros were painted this color in 1987. Anthony Young

The late-1980s standard, cloth, Camaro interior was handsome, comfortable, and provided superb in-the-saddle grip during vigorous handling exercises. The dash featured full instrumentation with few warning lights. Chevrolet

taking on anything from Europe in its price range. The editors at *Road & Track* felt the same, so they tested four factory hot rods from both here and abroad to determine a winner. The contestants were the Camaro IROC-Z, Pontiac Trans Am GTA, Toyota Supra, and Nissan 300ZX. The IROC-Z was the least expensive car in the group, with the Supra and 300ZX hovering around $20,000. The testing, which included long-distance travel, road course, and quarter-mile, proved just how superior the American cars were, and particularly the Camaro—it left the foreign competition in the weeds. Easily out-accelerating both the Supra and 300ZX, the IROC-Z also recorded the highest top speed of 150 miles per hour with its TPI 305-ci V-8, yet managed to achieve 23 miles per gallon in steady-state driving, thanks to its overdrive transmission. This powertrain in the IROC-Z was truly among the finest anywhere, and helped to make the Camaro IROC-Z among the finest performance cars in the world—at any price.

In spite of the car's many improvements, yet another recession dampened demand for the 1987 Camaros. Total sales were down to 137,760. Still,

Chevrolet had much to be proud of in its Camaro line. There were some additions and deletions to the 1988 line-up. The Z28 model was dropped as part of a rather confusing package option program that had begun in 1987. The base Camaro Sport Coupe and Sport Coupe convertible continued as before, but the next models were the IROC-Z Coupe and Convertible. There were now three levels of performance equipment standard or optional on the IROC-Z Coupe and the Convertible. The Base Group 1 was standard. Next came the Group 2 package, which was $1,846 on the Coupe and $1,747 on the Convertible. Group 3 cost $2,410 on the Coupe and $2,218 on the Convertible. Similar packages were offered on the base Sport Coupe and Sport Coupe convertible. These Groups were essentially packaged options that Chevrolet had found were most frequently ordered. It took considerable time poring over the Camaro brochure, and many questions to sales personnel, to learn what each package included.

This was the second year the 173-ci V-6 was the standard engine in the Sport Coupe. The trusty and popular four-cylinder was put out to pasture after 1986 came to an end. The V-6 reflected engine

CAMARO
1988 CHEVROLET

THE
Heartbeat
OF
AMERICA.
TODAY'S CHEVROLET

The 1988 Camaro brochure featured Chevrolet's hottest version: the IROC-Z. The Z28 was gone from the 1988 line-up and the IROC-Z was now a distinct model.

technology that was needed for the 1980s and beyond, was almost as fuel efficient, and provided better performance than the four-cylinder. There was also the 170-horsepower 305-ci V-8, which came standard in the Sport Coupe Convertible, but was optional in the Sport Coupe. The IROC-Z came standard with this engine, amazingly, but the optional engines included the LB9 TPI 195-horsepower 305 V-8 ($745) and the B2L TPI 230-horsepower 350-ci V-8 ($1,045).

The Camaro Sport Coupe and IROC-Z had by the late 1980s achieved a level of refinement and performance that made Chevrolet feel it had little further to do to the Camaro—and that was good. Chevrolet Division would now work on simply trying to boost its share of the market. It was a real quandary. By 1988, the Camaro was as good as technology and aesthetics could take it, yet sales were down to less than 97,000 units by the end of the model year. Chevrolet would spend the next four years trying to keep the Camaro flame alive until the fourth-generation Camaro would debut in 1993.

In 1988 Chevrolet replaced the four-barrel carburetor with a throttle body injector (TBI) on the 305-ci V-8 offered in Camaros. The TBI was mounted on a conventional cast-iron intake manifold. Engine RPO code was LO3. The rating was 170 horsepower at 4,000 rpm with 255 ft-lb of torque at 2,400 rpm. Faintly visible on the air cleaner cover are the words "Fuel Injection." Chevrolet

RADICAL AND REFINED

1 9 8 9 – 1 9 9 2

In the fall of 1988, President Ronald Reagan was completing his second term as one of the most popular presidents of the postwar era, albeit not without controversy. Vice President George W. Bush rode the Reagan coattails into the White House. America had recovered from the shock of the space shuttle *Challenger* explosion on January 28, 1986, and witnessed the successful launch of the shuttle *Discovery* 32 months later on September 29, 1988. The stock market had crashed on October 19, 1987, with hundreds of millions of dollars lost; it would take nearly two years to recover. Amidst this tumultuous decade, the Chevrolet Camaro carried on as one of the best performance cars in the world.

By the 1989 model year, the Camaro had reached a zenith in terms of looks and performance, but sales success eluded its grasp. The Camaro's greatest sales year had been 1979 with 282,571 sold. Another banner year was 1984, with over a

The RS Coupe became a regular model in the Camaro line in 1989, after successful sales of the car in targeted regions of North America in 1987 and 1988. The idea behind the RS was to borrow several styling aspects of the IROC-Z, most noticeably the ground effects pieces and handsome cast-aluminum wheels. Buyers agreed and bought over 83,000 RS Coupes in 1989. Chevrolet

production Camaro could excel. As sophisticated, refined, and powerful as the IROC-Z was as a street car, however, Showroom Stock racing had a way of bringing out the weaknesses in a car. The sanctioning bodies permitted changes to the shock absorbers or struts, wheels, and tires; no other changes to the suspension could be made. Racing the Camaros had revealed the brakes were the Achilles' heel. They were never designed to go from street to track.

Responding to complaints from Camaro racers, Phil Minch, a General Motors brake engineer, started casting about for a solution. The massive 12-inch front disc brakes off the Chevrolet Caprice used the same front bearing package as the Camaro. But the calipers, Minch suspected, would not be up to the task. After some research, Minch zeroed in on the two-piston aluminum caliper manufactured in Australia by PBR. This caliper was made for use on the Corvette and required modification to bolt to the Camaro spindle. Minch worked with Camaro platform chief engineer Chuck Hughes and F-car powertrain manager Ray Canale to get the car modified. The rear disc brakes that came with the original four-wheel disc brake option were felt to be adequate, since most of the braking force is borne by the front brakes. Bill Mitchell of Special Vehicle Developments was contracted to do track testing of the car. The stock front-to-rear proportioning valve was nonadjustable and did not work well with the new brake setup. It was replaced by a new proportioning valve with satisfactory results.

The vastly improved braking revealed another weakness. Under hard braking, the engine would suffer fuel starvation when the fuel level fell below a quarter tank. Baffles had to be added to the gas tank and a new fuel pickup and sock manufactured to ensure the tank-mounted fuel pump was constantly fed under all racing conditions.

Chevrolet addressed other complaints from racers. Virtually all the Camaros raced used the manual five-speed transmission. The overdrive fifth gear was

The standard V-8 in the 1990 IROC-Z was the 170-horsepower 305-ci LO3. Most buyers chose to upgrade to the more powerful 305-ci LB9 or the 350-ci B2L tuned-port V-8s. The B2L was available only in the IROC-Z Coupe and only with automatic transmission. David Newhardt

quarter of a million sold. Sales had ratcheted downward since then, and the total of less than 100,000 units sold in 1988 was discouraging. This time, Chevrolet Division did not feel that dialing in more horsepower would increase sales, because the IROC-Z was already a very hot performer, and a higher output V-8 would only drive up the price. The Camaro was such an aesthetic success, the division was very reluctant to change any sheet metal at all. The most prudent thing, the division felt, was to do practically nothing at all and just hang on until the new-generation Camaro was unveiled for 1993.

1LE: A Very Special Option

Not all was ho-hum with the Camaro for 1989, however. A new SCCA racing class had emerged in the late 1980s called Showroom Stock. It started in Canada first with the Canadian Players Challenge and grew to include SCCA and IMSA events in the United States. This was just the class where the top-of-the-line

great for mileage but too tall for the small-block V-8's torque and horsepower band. The Camaro racers were battling just to keep up with competing Mustangs, which were lighter and differently geared. It was decided to change the fifth gear ratio in those Camaros ordered with this trick racing component package. To further lower weight and revolving mass, an aluminum driveshaft would be part of the package. An engine oil cooler was also added as insurance.

An enthusiastic and competent engineering student, Mark Stielow, assisted Hughes and Canale in procuring the pieces for the 1LE option and getting them into the production loop so they could be assembled on the Van Nuys, California, assembly line. Chevrolet's John Heinracy, a frequent and successful racer of Corvettes and Camaros, was actively involved in the entire process from the racetrack to the Camaro assembly line to ensure the finished product performed back on the track. To qualify for Showroom Stock, all these new items had to be available on the production car so the car could, in fact, go Showroom Stock racing as equipped.

This special package was known in Chevrolet Engineering as 1LE, but it was not an RPO *per se*. The 1LE Special Performance Components Package was triggered when the G92 Performance Axle option was ordered and the C60 air conditioning option was *not* ordered. If only the G92 option was checked, the buyer had to select from the B2L 350-ci V-8 with automatic or the LB9 305-ci V-8 with five-speed manual. (The standard V-8 in the IROC-Z was the 170-horsepower LO3 305-ci V-8—not enough grunt for SCCA Showroom Stock competition.) The G92 package included the engine oil cooler, four-wheel disc brakes, dual converter exhausts, P245/50ZR16 Goodyear Eagle tires, a 145-mile per hour speedometer, and 5,500-rpm tachometer. Air conditioning could be ordered in these cars. If air conditioning was not ordered, this triggered the 1LE option code, which included the aluminum driveshaft, heavier duty front disc brakes and calipers, fuel tank baffle, specific front and rear shock absorbers, and unique durometer jounce bumpers. The 1LE option added nearly $700 to the car's price tag.

The 1LE Special Performance Components Package became available in mid-1988 but was virtually unknown to most Camaro racer-types; only four 1LE-equipped IROC-Zs were built at the Van Nuys plant that year. Soon, however, the performance grapevine was buzzing and for 1989 there were eager buyers

The familiar and distinctive taillight arrangement and IROC-Z badging identified this car as the top-performing Camaro.
David Newhardt

The door graphics and factory aluminum wheels make the late-1980s IROCs easy to spot on the street. David Newhardt

The no-nonsense layout of the instrument panel plainly relayed vital information to the driver. The large analog speedometer and tachometer were accompanied by oil pressure, volt meter, water temperature, and fuel level gauges.
David Newhardt

of America (SCCA) and International Motor Sports Association (IMSA) Showroom Stock series. Camaros won every race in the SCCA Escort Endurance Championship, and captured the 'Car of the Year' award in the IMSA's Firestone Firehawk series."

RS–The Rally Sport Returns

The RS had achieved respectable sales in the specific regions of America where it was sold— over 7,000 in 1988. Chevrolet decided to make it a regular model, replacing the Sport Coupe. The handsome ground effects package, cast aluminum wheels and other features of the RS package of 1988 and 1989 continued. Now, Camaro buyers all across the country and Canada could drive it too. The RS was available as a coupe and as a convertible, but did something unique in the area of powertrains. The coupe, which would sell in greater numbers, came standard with the 173-ci V-6. The convertible was offered with the 170-horsepower 305 V-8; this engine was available as an option in the RS Coupe and was standard in the IROC-Z coupe and convertible.

ready with checkbooks in-hand. The dual-cat exhaust system was added to the package that year. A total of 111 IROC-Zs were ordered with this package. And the buyers were not disappointed. Chevrolet writes, "In 1989, Chevy's F-body swept the Sports Car Club

Buyers could not go the "econo-racer" route and order the LB9 195-horsepower TPI 305 for $745 in the $11,495 RS Coupe. The B2L 230-horsepower TPI

This 1990 IROC-Z carries the Custom Cloth interior. High-back bucket seats with adjustable head restraints helped make for a comfortable ride. Interiors were available in standard cloth-and-vinyl, optional Custom Cloth, and Custom Leather seating surfaces.
David Newhardt

350 ($1,045) was also out of the question. These engines could only be ordered as options in the IROC-Z coupe or convertible. Nevertheless, the RS Coupe and Convertible proved to be just what the market wanted. Nearly 83,500 RS Coupes were sold, but the $16,995 RS Convertible drew only 3,245 buyers.

IROC, I-Roll

The exotic 1LE package was deliberately hidden, it seemed, within the esoteric option structure Chevrolet had established. It was not for every IROC-Z buyer, but only those who took seriously the desire to go Showroom Stock racing. Not all 1LE-equipped IROC-Zs went racing. Some buyers, sensing the possibility of future collectability, ordered their cars with the G92/1LE package simply for the joy of having them and driving them on the street while basking in the cachet of having a 1LE. The few Camaros so ordered and driven only on the street were mostly sold in northern states where the lack of air conditioning was not a hardship. Still, for most buyers of the IROC-Z, the car's capabilities were perfect for streets all across the North American continent. Ignorance of the 1LE package, in this case, was bliss. Americans had come to expect air conditioning

The liftback on the Camaro allowed access to a sizable storage compartment. With the rear seat folded down, the Camaro hardtops had a 31-cubic-foot capacity.
David Newhardt

in their cars, and few IROC-Z buyers were willing to live without it.

The Camaro's V-8 powerplants were in good shape. As mentioned, the LB9 305-ci V-8 with optional MX0 automatic overdrive transmission

In 1988 the IROC-Z became a distinct model in the Camaro line and the Z28 moniker was dropped. The 1990 model was virtually identical to the 1988 model. This pristine 1990 example, finished in Code 41 Black was one of 22,243 IROC-Zs built in 1990.
David Newhardt

The 305-ci 170-horsepower LO3 V-8 was standard in the IROC-Z for 1988 and 1989. It featured throttle-body injection, or TBI, instead of a carburetor. TBI was designed to operate using sophisticated electronic engine controls. Most IROC-Z buyers, however, opted for the more powerful tuned-port 305- or 350-ci small-block V-8. Chevrolet

delivered 195 horsepower. With the standard five-speed manual transmission and standard single exhaust, the engine was rated at 220 horsepower. With optional dual exhaust the engine gained an extra 10 horsepower. The venerable 350-ci small-block V-8 had remained in production for more than 20 years, although it suffered a brief absence from the Camaro for several years, as a result of Chevrolet's efforts to meet CAFE standards. Chevrolet had surmounted the CAFE hurdle through the use of emerging technology—TPI—and the mandatory option of automatic transmission. Doing this allowed the 350 to skirt the dreaded gas-guzzler tax, which was a stigma Chevrolet would not accept or pay for. The B2L returned for its third year of production. With the single exhaust system it developed 230 horsepower; with dual exhaust it pumped out 240 horses.

Sales of Camaros in 1989 picked up 15 percent over 1988 with a total of 110,739 sold. The following year the car's fortunes would reverse, and the Camaro would go through yet another near-death experience.

A "Z" by Any Other Name

Chevrolet's involvement with the International Race of Champions and its licensing agreement with the organization ended at the close of 1989. No 1990 IROC-Zs could be built after December 31, 1989. What would Chevrolet do for a high-performance Camaro after that date? Actually, IROC-Z was

The tuned-port injection (TPI) 305-ci LB9 and 350-ci B2L V-8s were the hot tickets to power the IROC-Z and Z28 in the late 1980s and early 1990s. During this period, output of these two engines increased as engineers made further improvement in engine controls and exhaust. The engines also marked the pinnacle of performance engine aesthetics, as GM Powertrain worked to make the engines look as powerful as they were. Chevrolet

merely a name; it was the car and its underpinnings that counted. Management discussed reviving the Z28 badge but this might cause confusion in the market when mixed with IROC-Zs in the 1990 model year. Chevrolet's Jim Perkins decided to shorten the 1990 model run and accelerate the introduction of the 1991 models. Production of the 1990 models began in mid-September as usual and the RS and IROC-Z coupes and convertibles for 1990 would be built until the end of the year. These Camaros would remain in the sales pipeline while Chevrolet made the mild changes needed for the 1991 models to be introduced in March of 1990.

Chevrolet had a new, larger displacement V-6 in the RS, with displacement bumped to 191 cubic inches and horsepower rated at 140. The 170-horsepower 305 was still standard in the RS Convertible. There were no earth-shaking changes under the hood but the 350-ci B2L V-8 was now blessed with a true dual converter exhaust system, raising output to 245 horsepower. Still no five-speed tranny, as the overdrive automatic was the only transmission available bolted to this engine. The 305 LB9 was rated at 210 horsepower.

With the introduction of the 1990 models, Chevrolet marked more than 35 years of continuous small-block V-8 production. Millions of these engines had been built. It remained the engine of choice for countless Chevrolet enthusiasts. The small-block had not only survived, it had prospered. Louis Cuttitta retired from Chevrolet in 1986 after more than 30 years of work on the small-block. In 1990, he explained this V-8's success and longevity:

"The small-block V-8 is a simple engine made with inexpensive materials. That's why it has lived so long. And it's practically indestructible. Any idiot can do things to it without hurting it. You can let it run low on oil and it seems to last a long time. In fact, did you know a Chevrolet V-8 with no oil in it and no water in it, running wide-open throttle, will last about two hours before it disintegrates? We did it twice. The first time it lasted an hour and 15 minutes and the second time it lasted two hours."

Regardless who is asked, virtually every Chevrolet engineer who has ever worked on the small-block V-8 during his career has the utmost respect for the engine. Although he retired from Chevrolet in 1983, Dick Keinath still has the greatest admiration for the

powerplant conceived by Ed Cole and Harry Barr, and executed by Al Kolbe, Don McPherson, and many others.

"I have always liked the small-block," Keinath said in 1990. "I've enjoyed working with it. It's been a good engine. It was innovative at the time and because it was so innovative, it's still right up there in front. All we've done in the last [nearly] 40 years is to refine it and keep it current. It's been an engine that's been most responsive to anything an engineer wanted to do. I would call it an engineer's engine. Because of that, it's been a joy to work on, and it's been interesting to work on. You could get from it what you expected to get from it, either design-wise, durability-wise or induction-wise. It was an engine that would respond very favorably to what you were trying to do to it. That is why it was always an engine that we enjoyed improving on. I don't think in all the annals of automotive history you'll ever find another one where that can be said of the engine."

It was the 305- and 350-ci V-8 that carried the small-block mantle into the 1990s. Technology had not only given the small-block new life, it had given it renewed performance. And the level of performance

The TPI V-8s were assembled at GM's famed Flint, Michigan, engine plant, where workers literally gave the engines the white glove treatment during assembly. Two assemblers are finishing installation of the induction system on 350-ci TPI V-8s destined for the Corvette. **Chevrolet**

Above and below: The IROC-Z convertible for 1989 was a rare commodity, with fewer than 4,000 built. Chevrolet participation in the IROC series would continue in 1990, but was to end abruptly. Without license to use the IROC name on its car, Chevrolet brought back the Z28 for 1991.

rivaled the figures Chevrolet enthusiasts routinely read about in road tests during the 1960s. *Motor Trend* tested a 1990 IROC-Z for the March 1990 issue, equipped with the TPI 350-ci V-8, automatic transmission, and 3.23:1 axle ratio. The editors wrote, "The IROC is blazingly fast out of the hole. The 2.2-second 0–30 mile per hour acceleration is one of the best we've *ever* tested, ranking right up there with the likes of the Porsche 911 Carrera 4, Chevy Corvette, and Lotus Esprit Turbo."

Motor Trend also tested two 1LE-equipped IROC-Zs, one with the 305 and the other with the 350. These two cars proved just how close the performance was

between the B2L and LB9 TPI V-8s. The TPI 305 V-8 was rated at 230 horsepower at 4,400 rpm with 300 lb-ft of torque at 3,200 rpm. It was mated to the five-speed manual transmission with 3.42:1 rear axle. The TPI 350 was rated at 245 horsepower at 4,400 rpm with 345 ft-lb of torque at 3,200 rpm and hooked up to the automatic transmission with 3.23 rear end. Both engines had a 9.3:1 compression ratio.

The TPI 305 IROC-Z reached 60 miles per hour in 6.3 seconds and covered the quarter-mile in 14.8 seconds at 95.4 miles per hour. The other car with the TPI 350 reached 60 miles per hour in 6.1 seconds and covered the quarter-mile in 14.8 seconds doing 96 miles per hour. Not only did the TPI 305 get better highway mileage than the larger displacement small-block, it also gave virtually identical performance.

With performance levels like these, which matched or bested any street cars the division built in the 1960s, Chevrolet rightly saw no need to boost performance. The goal of restoring truly stirring acceleration while meeting the tough emissions and fuel economy requirements had been achieved.

Perhaps the most significant change to the Camaro for 1990 was one that could not be seen. Federal regulations mandated a passive restraint for the driver—in other words, an airbag. All 1990 model cars had to be so equipped. General Motors had spent millions of dollars on research and development of its Supplemental Inflatable Restraint systems for all the

cars in its divisions. Despite the added cost of this safety feature, the price of the RS Coupe and Convertible actually dropped. The price of the IROC-Z Coupe and Convertible rose considerably, however. In fact, the price of the Convertible now topped $20,000. There were other new standard features on the 1990 Camaros that had previously been options. These included tilt steering column, tinted glass, intermittent wipers, and halogen headlights.

Due to a crippling UAW strike in 1990, the figures are misleading. Only 34,986 Camaros were built for this model year. Of these, 28,750 were RS Coupes, 729 were RS Convertibles, 4,213 were IROC-Z Coupes, and 1,294 were IROC-Z Convertibles. Only 62 cars were equipped with the 1LE option.

The 1991 Camaros were massaged aesthetically if not mechanically. Both RS and Z28 models featured new ground-effects panels with implied air scoops in front of both front and rear wheelwell openings. The Z28 featured a new, taller airfoil-type rear spoiler, while the RS retained the low-profile rear spoiler. There was a new high-mount stoplight mounted to the hatch glass; the convertible had the additional stoplight integrated with the spoiler. All the powertrains for 1990 were carried over unchanged for 1991. There was, however, a new option that created some fresh performance possibilities for individuals—or police departments—on a budget.

The B4C Special Service Package

Full-size Chevrolets had always appealed to local and state police departments for their interior room. By the end of the 1980s, however, the Caprice simply was not available with the high-output V-8s that were needed for pursuit work. Neither the TPI 305 nor 350 were available in the Caprice. Chevrolet responded to complaints heard from police departments by offering the Special Service Package on the Camaro RS Coupe for 1991. The option code for this was B4C. It was basically a Z28 in RS trim.

Above and below: Designers specified considerable door sill and underbody reinforcement to be added during the conversion from coupe to convertible. The cloth top was not electrically powered, and had to be raised and lowered manually. However, it was so well designed that lowering or raising the top took only seconds.

For those who wanted to take their Z28 showroom stock racing, it helped to be on good terms with the local Chevrolet dealer. A complex formula was involved when ordering the 1LE Special Performance Components Package that was essential for racing. Formal production availability of 1LE began in 1989. This 1991 Z28 with the 1LE package was one of 478 built that year. It is owned by Gregg Blakely of Arlington, Texas. **Anthony Young**

The B4C option cost $3,135 on top of the RS Coupe base list price of $12,180. It included the G92 Performance Axle package, which necessitated the choice of the LB9 305 with five-speed manual transmission or the B2L 350 with automatic transmission. The B4C option with the 350 V-8 cost $3,950. With either engine, the dual catalytic converter exhaust system was included, along with air conditioning, 16-inch aluminum wheels mounted with 245/50ZR16 tires, four-wheel disc brakes, engine oil cooler, 105-amp alternator, heavy-duty 630 amp battery, 145-mile per hour speedometer, Z28 suspension, and the limited-slip 3.23:1 differential. To be sure, the B4C-equipped Camaros did not come equipped with the Z28 hood blisters or high-profile rear spoiler.

These cars were a revelation to those police departments that bought them and the officers who drove them. They were no longer left in the dust but could easily pursue and overtake just about any car on the road, except maybe the Corvette or another Z28! Law enforcement journals began writing about the B4C Camaros and soon local and state police departments began including them in their annual budget requests. In 1991 a total of 592 B4C Camaros were ordered. Of course, those eagle-eyed Camaro sleuths who discovered the 1LE option soon unearthed the B4C Special Service Package. Stealth Performance was born.

Blakely's 1LE Z28 has an interesting history, as most 1LEs usually do. This car was among several ordered by a dealer in Dallas, Texas, who planned to take them SCCA racing. The dealer never got around to racing this one, so it was moved to the lot. Since 1LEs could not be ordered with A/C, this one sat on the lot for over a year and was finally sold in 1992. The first owner decided to sell it in 1997, and Blakely snapped it up. Anthony Young

1992–Camaro's 25th Anniversary

When the 1992 Camaros were introduced in the fall of 1989, Chevrolet celebrated a quarter-century of Camaro production. It did so by offering the Heritage Package, RPO Z03. It was available on all Camaro models, and included hood and rear deck stripes, black headlight pockets, a matching-color grille, and a 25th anniversary badge. The last production year of the third generation Camaro was received by the automotive press with admiration for what been accomplished over the previous decade. At the same time, the magazine editors were relieved that the third-generation Camaro was ceasing production. It had gone as far as Chevrolet could take it with the existing platform. The small-block V-8 also had to adapt to the challenges in the 1990s and there were numerous improvements that could be made to this engine, including new fuel delivery systems, induction design, electronic engine controls, and exhaust emission controls.

A total of 70,007 Camaros were sold in 1992. No doubt many prospective Camaro buyers held off buying a 1992 model in anticipation of the all-new Camaro scheduled for 1993. Those who did decide to wait were not disappointed.

The 1991 Z28 coupes received the new, high-profile rear spoiler. A total of 12,452 Z28 Coupes were built that year. Blakely's car is finished in Code 98 Ultra Blue. No exterior identification was added for the 1LE package. For collectors of Camaros like this one, the build sheet is everything. Anthony Young

The Chevrolet TPI 305-ci and 350-ci V-8s rank among the finest engines of the late 1980s and early 1990s. They have superb horsepower and torque characteristics. This is the engine compartment of Blakely's 1LE Z28 with B2L V-8.

CHAPTER 8

THE FOURTH GENERATION IS LAUNCHED

1 9 9 3 – 1 9 9 5

B y the 1990s, the Camaro had become one of the most enduring cars by Chevrolet or any other automaker. The Camaro had survived and adapted to the demands of the market and the federal government. It entered its fourth generation having witnessed the psychedelic 1960s, the funky 1970s, and the Me Decade—the 1980s. By 1993, the Camaro was well into what would ultimately be called the scandalous 1990s.

The Camaro survived these tumultuous decades because it remained true to its original concept, a vision that was universal from decade to decade. That concept was a sporty four-place two-door passenger car with handsome, enduring styling coupled with excellent handling and impressive performance—all at an affordable price. There are numerous examples of cars that started with a great concept but changed over time to bear no resemblance to their origins and ultimately died in the marketplace. Two examples are the Ford Thunderbird and the Dodge Charger.

The excellent design of the fourth-generation Camaro made it appear smaller than the third-generation car. In fact, overall dimensions were almost identical.
David Newhardt

123

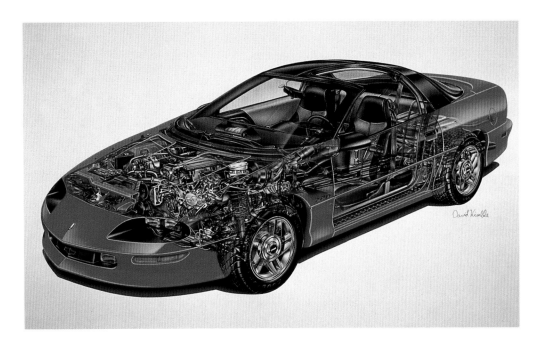

models in its line-up. Besides, Chevrolet knew and Camaro buyers knew real performance meant rear-wheel drive. That fact was also true of race cars and the Camaro continued to race successfully in numerous series all across North America. If the new Camaro switched to front-wheel drive all this racing activity would disappear, along with the income generated from it. All the private and corporate racing efforts that kept the "Race on Sunday, Sell on Monday" market presence would also vanish. Simply put, the rear-wheel drive Camaro was here to stay, for very sound engineering and marketing reasons.

The introduction of each new-generation Camaro inevitably was followed by praise for the new car's looks. The fourth-generation Camaro elicited perhaps the greatest amount of positive press Chevrolet had ever seen. Chevrolet's exterior and interior design studios made the new Camaro a visually stunning success. The sleek new design was an aesthetic triumph. There was not a single bad line on the car.

In December 1992 Chevrolet's Public Relations Department issued a press release that said:

"In the 1960s, muscle cars were like the muscle men of the era: formidable, hulking presences dominated by brute strength. But the science of muscle has come a long way since then. Like today's bodybuilders, the 1993 Camaro is lean, finely proportioned and powerful. It's a muscle car for the Nineties."

David Kimble, renowned for his cutaway renderings, did this one of the 1993 Camaro Z28. To do this rendering, Kimble was allowed secret access to the new Camaro design long before the public ever saw the car. **Chevrolet**

Introducing the Fourth Generation

Spy photos leaked to *Automotive Week* in 1992 showed the new Camaro appearing smaller, and once again the front-wheel prognosticators speculated on the drivetrain. Chevrolet now had a mix of front- and rear-wheel drive cars. Would the new Camaro make the switch?

The automotive pundits were forgetting Chevrolet knew its market for the Camaro oh-so-well. The division was not about to gamble on a completely new drive-train configuration on one of the longest-running

Kimble's rendering of the new Camaro chassis shows a wealth of detail. Chevrolet departed from the live axle and leaf spring rear suspension to a new design incorporating trailing lower control arms, lateral link, and coil springs. **Chevrolet**

"Completely redesigned from nose to tail, the fourth-generation Camaro wears a sculptured, contemporary skin over hardware that's been thoroughly updated to meet the needs of today's most demanding sports-car enthusiasts. All the classic Camaro design ingredients are evident—the smooth upper body, tenacious stance, aggressive front-end treatment and brawny wheels and tires—yet the look is fresh and strikingly contemporary."

Among the driving aesthetic elements of the new design is the windshield angle. The angle on the new Camaro was 68 degrees. This measurement actually harkens back to the days when automobiles had vertical windshields. This steeply raked windshield created packaging challenges, not the least of which was engine and component installation and subsequent service. During preliminary designs, it became clear the base of the windshield would actually cover a portion of the engine, both V-6 and V-8. The induction systems of both engines planned for the Camaro would have to clear the windshield with space to spare.

While spy photos of the new Camaro gave the appearance of a downsized F-body, the car was actually longer, wider, and taller! The Camaro still rode on the same 101-inch wheelbase as before, but the beautifully crafted exterior was so well executed the increased exterior dimensions could not be discerned. The entire car had been engineered and designed on computers, but the computer models had been heavily influenced by the rendering and clay modeling efforts of the design studios. The Fisher Body Division of General Motors was pioneering the use of sheet molded compound (SMC) body panels made of chopped fiberglass and polyester resin. The new Camaro would use SMC for the roof, doors, hatch, and spoiler assembly. The Reaction Injection Molded (RIM) process would be used for the front fenders and fascia. The rear fascia would be reinforced polyurethane. There was some sheet metal used on the new Camaro. The hood and rear quarter panels were galvanized steel.

Chevrolet took a new approach for the front and rear suspension of the G4 Camaro. The front suspension was a refinement of the previous unequal-length control arms setup, which Chevrolet called short and long (control) arm—SLA—suspension. The upper arm was mounted high in the body structure

by a "gooseneck" knuckle to reduce loads. The integral coil-over-shock featured a monotube de Carbon high gas-pressure shock absorber. The front spring rate for the RS would be 38 N-mm (Newtons per millimeter) and 51 N/mm for the Z28. The front stabilizer bar, referred to as a stabilizer shaft, was actually a 30-millimeter diameter tube to save weight.

The rear suspension featured a traditional live axle, but used a multilink axle design using two trailing lower control arms, torque arm, tie rod, and tie rod brace. The coil springs were damped using high gas-pressure de Carbon monotube shocks. The standard spring rate was 16.7 N/mm and 19.9 N/mm for the Z28. The solid steel rear stabilizer bar was 17 millimeters for the Coupe and 19 millimeters for the Z28. The Coupe came with front disc and rear drum brakes with GM's antilock brake system (ABS). The Z28 featured four-wheel disc brakes with ABS, having 10.9-inch by 1.28-inch front discs and 11.4-inch by 0.8-inch rear discs.

The 1LE package was minimized on the fourth generation Z28. The aluminum driveshaft was no longer included in the package. The package did include larger 32-millimeter front and 21-millimeter rear stabilizer bars with higher-rate bushings, higher-rate front upper and lower control arm bushings, stiffer front and rear shock valving with the rear de Carbon monotube shock bore diameter increased from 36 millimeters to 46 millimeters, and retention

The Camaro Coupe was the most affordable model in the 1993 line, with a base list under $14,000. In terms of style, it ranks as one of the greatest automotive designs of the 1990s. **Chevrolet**

The standard powerplant in the 1993 Camaro Coupe was the L32 3.4-liter V-6. It received a boost in power that year to 160 horsepower, with more horsepower per cubic inch than the small-block V-8s of the early 1980s. **Chevrolet**

of the radiator baffles included with air conditioning systems in Camaros. The A/C system itself, however, was not installed.

Chevrolet had been working on what it called the Gen II small-block V-8. This V-8 was to display numerous improvements in terms of combustion

chamber design, induction design, coolant flow, more sophisticated ignition, and better engine sealing. At the same time, an even more powerful high-performance small-block V-8 was also being engineered to power first the Corvette, and then the Z28. That engine was given a legendary RPO.

The LT1 V-8

In the late 1980s, the engineers at Chevrolet and GM Powertrain began work on significant changes on the small-block to further improve performance, fuel economy, emissions, and durability. These changes would allow Chevrolet to offer the engine well into the next century. The changes and improvements envisioned were so comprehensive, the project was given the name Gen II. Nevertheless, a small-block it would remain. Chevrolet realized that discarding the proven small-block platform for something new would be a mistake.

The company focused its attention on improving the performance of the L98, the base 350-ci V-8 in the Corvette. As mentioned earlier, Tuned Port Injection was originally developed for the 305-ci V-8. While the TPI 350 was a vast improvement over the Cross Fire Injection 350, it was not ideal. The engineers at Chevrolet felt the TPI L98 could be improved upon.

The interior of the new Camaro was as well thought out and designed as the exterior. The emphasis was on gauges with a minimum of warning lights. **Chevrolet**

Anil Kulkarni of GM Powertrain was chief engineer for the project. Research and development was focused on these key areas: induction (including cylinder heads), coolant flow, ignition, and exhaust. As with any project of this nature, it was a closely guarded secret and details of this engine were not released until the long-lead Corvette press preview in the summer of 1991 in Montreal, Canada. The press also learned the LT1 would be offered in the forthcoming Camaro for 1993.

At the Montreal press preview, when the hoods were raised on the 1992 Corvettes, the automotive press saw an engine radically different in appearance from the L98 that had powered the Corvette since 1985 and the TPI small-blocks in the Camaro since 1986. Gone were the induction plenum, tubes, and manifold that had become familiar during the previous seven years. They were replaced by a low-rise, one-piece cast-aluminum intake manifold. This new intake manifold eliminated the water crossover between the cylinder heads, effectively lowering the overall height of the engine by 3.50 inches. Coupled to the intake manifold was a new throttle body and low-restriction air snorkle. The high-pressure fuel rail on each side of the manifold fed gas to the AC Rochester Multec fuel injectors. These injectors showed an improvement over previous units by giving more precise fuel flow and a spray pattern matched to this specific engine's output.

The editors and writers noticed another feature of this new engine—the High Energy Ignition (HEI) housing at the rear of the engine was gone. In its place was a new optical sensor-type ignition at the front of the engine. A new precision-cast and machined aluminum front cover housed the new gear-driven water pump and optical distributor. The distributor housing featured a stainless steel shutter wheel that was driven by a shaft off the camshaft sprocket. Light shining through this shutter wheel produced 360 pulses per crankshaft revolution. These signals were fed to the Powertrain Control Module, which precisely issued the spark timing commands. The net result of this effort was the most precise ignition timing, which reduced emissions, improved power, and optimized fuel economy.

A major feature of this new engine—dubbed the LT1 after its legendary predecessor—was its reverse-flow cooling system. The system was designed to

route coolant first through the cylinder heads after making a brief passage through the engine block to better cool the cylinder head and intake manifold. It then passes to the engine block and around the cylinder bores, and finally back to the water pump before it repeats the procedure or is directed to the radiator. The gear-driven water pump was designed to eliminate the constant side load on the bearings and seals of standard water pumps that eventually results in leaks. The reverse-flow concept necessitated redesigning the engine block and cylinder heads extensively, so these major components are unique to the LT1 and were not interchangeable with earlier small-blocks. Reverse-flow cooling produced uniform cylinder bore temperatures and reduced ring bore friction, reducing wear and increasing mileage.

The cylinder heads received extensive research and development in the intake and exhaust port to improve flow. This was carefully matched to the design of the intake and exhaust manifolds. Intake and exhaust valve diameter was unchanged from the L98—1.94 and 1.50 inches respectively. For this engine, Chevrolet returned to cast-iron exhaust manifolds, doing away with the steel tube headers fitted to the L98.

Performance of the LT1 was improved even further with revised camshaft specifications. Intake and exhaust valve lift were both 0.450-inch, compared to

The Z28 featured contrasting black roof and exterior mirrors with a choice of body colors. Subtle Z28 badging appeared on the front fenders and rear facia. **Chevrolet**

The fourth-generation Camaro featured integral rear spoiler with high-mount stop lamp. The new Camaro exhibited one of the lowest drag coefficients of GM's entire fleet of cars. **Chevrolet**

the L98's 0.415-inch for the intake and 0.430-inch for the exhaust. The exhaust system was designed to improve flow and reduce emissions even further. The LT1 in the Z28 was rated at 275 horsepower at 5,000 rpm with 326 ft-lb of torque at 2,400 rpm. This engine differed in a number of ways from the LT1 installed in the Corvette. The LT1 in the Z28 came with a single catalytic converter exhaust system, where the LT1 in the Corvette came with a dual cat/dual exhaust system. The exhaust manifolds on the Z28 differed from those on the Corvette V-8. In addition, the accessory drives were located in different places and the valve covers on the Z28 LT1 were stamped steel, while the Corvette engine used black composite covers. The port injectors were exposed on the Z28 engine, while the Corvette LT1 was equipped with "beauty panels" to cover the injectors. Both engines had air injection reaction pumps, but the Corvette had the pump mounted to the engine block, while the LT1 in the Z28 had the pump mounted on the left side of the engine bay. The LT1 naturally had a higher output, rated at 300 horsepower.

A New High Output V-6

The LT1 did not steal all the performance thunder. The 1993 Camaro Coupe came standard with the most powerful V-6 Chevrolet had ever offered in passenger cars up to that time. The L32 V-6 was a new

overhead valve 3.4-liter engine with output that rivaled the output of the small-block V-8s installed in the Z28 in the late 1970s and early 1980s. This engine was rated at 160 horsepower at 4,600 rpm with 200 ft-lb. of torque at 3,600 rpm. This exceeds the output of the LG4 305-ci V-8 having 145–155 horsepower as installed in the 1982–86 Z28, and it matched the 350-ci LM1 V-8 put in Z28s shipped to California in the late 1970s. In terms of power-to-weight ratio, the 1993 Camaro Coupe had the Z28 of the late 1970s and early 1980s beat.

Chevrolet implemented a "family strategy" to make as many components as possible common to both the LT1 and the L32 engines in an effort to reduce engine manufacturing and service cost. This resulted in the use of a common air conditioning compressor and air cleaner, a similar accessory drive (with shared connections and attachments), and identical crank and rod bearing fits. The changes improved the engine and vehicle assembly process as well as serviceability at the dealerships.

The L32 featured Sequential Port Fuel Injection (SFI) with more powerful engine control module (ECM), a direct ignition system similar to that developed for the LT1. For the new Camaro, the previous three-piece intake manifold of the 3.1-liter V-6 was replaced with a two-piece cast-aluminum design that lowered the engine's profile and reduced the number of parts and overall mass as well.

Camaro Coupe buyers were highly interested in fuel economy, and the L32 V-6 delivered here as well. Both city and highway mileage EPA ratings were up for both manual transmission and automatic-equipped Camaros. The L32-equipped cars delivered identical mileage with either the manual or automatic transmission— 19.0 EPA estimated city miles per gallon and 28 miles per gallon on the highway.

The Press Weighs In

"The sound alone is worth the price of admission: Whoever tuned the exhaust on the new LT1-powered Camaro Z28 deserves a bonus." So wrote Matt DeLorenzo in the May 10, 1993, issue of *AutoWeek.* That opening line pretty much set the tone for the entire article. It was not a full-fledged road test but a one-page column titled simply "Driving Impressions." As the saying goes, however, first impressions are the most important. Editors, who

often test cars on a daily basis, can get blasé as one new car often feels and drives like all the rest. Not so with the fourth-generation Z28. The new Z was an order of magnitude above the previous generation car in terms of acceleration, ride, and even handling.

The B4C Special Service Package and the 1LE option were available on the new-generation Camaros. However, the 1LE fourth-generation cars no longer included the aluminum driveshaft that had been part of the option on the third-generation Z28. There was also an Indianapolis 500 Pace Car Replica option, RPO B5A, to commemorate the Camaro's selection, again, as the pace car for the legendary race. This $995 option was the most striking pace car design ever seen on a Camaro. It included a black-over-white paint scheme separated by several colorful ribbons running from nose to tail. The cast-aluminum wheels were painted white. The interior continued the theme with specially designed seat fabric. There was, of course, Indy 500 identification on the doors, but mercifully smaller than had been done in the past. A total of 633 Pace Car Replicas were sold.

Despite all the rave reviews of the new Camaro, the sales figures for 1993 were low. As with any new model, problems that arose during production had to be resolved and this often slowed weekly production from the Camaro's Ste. Therese, Quebec, Canada, assembly plant. The fact that the Chevrolet Camaro was no longer assembled in America was not a fact that the division emphasized. Certainly, Chevrolet management was concerned about whether this would bother Camaro buyers, but the company covered its bases by conducting focus groups covering a wide variety of prospective buyers. The consensus was that it was not a big issue. By the time the last 1993 Camaro rolled off the assembly line outside Montreal, total production for the year was 39,103. Of these, 21,253 were Coupes and 17,850 were Z28s.

The new LT1 350-ci V-8 powered the 1993 Z28. With a net rating of 275 horsepower, it was capable of pushing the Z28 to 150 miles per hour. The cylinder block and heads were completely redesigned to improve airflow and provide more efficient cooling. **Chevrolet**

The 1993 Z28 served as pace car for the Indianapolis 500 that year. The paint scheme was a complete departure from the simple striping of previous Camaro pace cars. **Chevrolet**

The Camaro Convertible was introduced in 1994 to an eagerly awaiting market, but it was nearly $5,000 more than the Coupe. Unlike the previous generation Camaro convertible, which was a conversion by an outside vendor, Chevrolet built this new convertible on the same Canadian assembly line as the Coupe. **Chevrolet**

The Sun Shines In–Again

Noticeably absent from the Camaro line-up in 1993 was a convertible. From the moment the fourth-generation Camaro was being rendered and modeled in clay, a convertible was in the plans. Rather than have the convertible produced by a conversion company, the new Camaro convertible would be manufactured by Chevrolet. Here the power of computer technology was thoroughly applied. Using an approach called finite element analysis, engineers could replicate the stresses on the convertible body/chassis structure as had been done with the Coupe. The computer programs could be used to determine the sort of strengthening the convertible required to minimize the "shake, rattle, and roll" encountered in previous generations of Camaro convertibles. All the engineering, tooling, and manufacturing planning involved in the new convertible created practically a whole new vehicle program. This was the reason the convertible was delayed by a year.

With its extra reinforcements and soft top hardware, the convertible was heavier than the coupe. The new convertible weighed 3,350 pounds. Portions of the car's unibody construction were of heavier gauge steel and there were other reinforcements that made this the most structurally rigid Camaro ever built. It was also the quietest and best-handling droptop Camaro ever. But that wind-in-the-hair pleasure came with a price tag. Base list price of the Camaro Convertible was $18,475. The average "price as tested" often topped $22,000. Perhaps that is why only 2,328 were sold in 1994.

The Z28 was also available as a convertible. Price of the Z28 Coupe was now just under $17,000 and the Convertible listed for $22,075. Still, the powerful and refined LT1 V-8 made the Z28s an absolute blast to drive, and among the fastest cars in the world—certainly at this price. The standard LT1 now featured Sequential Port Fuel Injection, or SFI for short. This system appeared first on the V-6, and was now on the LT1. Horsepower remained the same at 275 ponies. Coupled to the LT1 was a new six-speed manual transmission featuring Computer Aided Gear Selection (CAGS). During low to medium acceleration from a stop, the CAGS performed a skip-shift from first gear to fourth to improve fuel economy and emissions. The torque of the LT1 made this possible. Under pedal-to-the-metal acceleration, you still experienced the thrill of winding the small-block V-8 through every gear. The sixth gear was also designed to get the highest possible highway mileage so the Z28 could skirt the gas-guzzler tax. There was also a new four-speed automatic transmission with more sophisticated electronic controls designed to maximize mileage and minimize emissions.

Weekend racers could still order the 1LE package on their Z28s (135 did so), and the local constabulary could also order up the B4C Special Service Package. Chevrolet sold 668 of the latter—not all of them to police departments! Total Camaro sales for 1994 were 119,799. This was the best sales year since 1987.

Gen 4, Year 3

Prospective Camaro buyers were really warming up to the fourth-generation car. The most popular car in the line was the V-6 Coupe, and Chevrolet focused its engineering development on an optional V-6 with even more power. The new engine introduced in the 1995 Camaro was a 3.8-liter V-6. In the Camaro this powerplant was mounted longitudinally to permit rear-wheel drive, but engineers designed the engine to power other GM automobiles mounted transversely for front-wheel drive. The L36 3.8-liter

1995
C A M A R O

Chevrolet printed a separate brochure for the Special Service Package, which could be ordered using RPO B4C. This car became the ultimate pursuit vehicle of choice with state and local police departments in the 1990s.

V-6 was rated at 200 net horsepower at 5,200 rpm with 225 ft-lb of torque at 4,000 rpm. Unfortunately, it was only available with the four-speed automatic transmission, but Chevrolet promised the five-speed manual would be offered in the near future. The optional L36 was available in both the Coupe and Convertible for $350. Over 4,700 buyers selected this powerful V-6.

The Z28 for 1995 received only subtle refinements. There was a new option, RPO NW9, called Acceleration Slip Regulation (ASR). This was originally developed for the Corvette, and was now available on the Z28. This

1994 CHEVROLET CAMARO CONVERTIBLE

The 1994 Camaro Convertible graced the cover of this piece of Chevrolet literature. Standard power for 1994 was a 3.4-liter V-6 engine. The Z28 powerplant was the 5.7-liter LT1 V-8. Chevrolet

equipment, installed on the LT1, limited the amount of accelerator travel when it sensed tire spin. Many drivers stated it was a strange sensation to feel the pedal actually push against the driver's foot under hard acceleration with the ASR engaged. It could be turned off if the driver wanted to smoke the tires.

Output of the LT1 remained unchanged. On the outside, however, Z28 buyers had new choices in the color combination. Since 1993, the Z28 had been offered in a two-tone color scheme: a black roof and C-pillar combined with a choice of body colors. For 1995, there was a monochromatic no-charge option, RPO D82, with the roof and body all one color. It was a popular option, chosen by over 17,000 buyers of the Z28 Coupe.

Prices of the 1995 Camaros picked up right along with increased sales. The Coupe, listing for $14,250, was the best seller at 77,431. The Camaro Convertible listed for $19,495 and was snapped up by 6,948 buyers. The Z28 Coupe listed for $17,915 and was purchased by 30,335 enthusiasts. The Z28 Convertible, the most expensive Camaro of the group, listed for $23,095. A respectable 8,024 buyers drove one home. Total Camaro sales for 1995 came to 122,738.

This 1994 ad didn't mince words. With 275 horsepower, 325 lb-ft of torque under the hood, a much stiffer chassis, and ABS brakes, the 1994 Z28 could challenge and beat most of the domestic sports car competition. Chevrolet

Chevrolet continued the B4C and 1LE special options, and there were other considerations for buyers as well. In Massachusetts, Camaro buyers had to purchase a mandatory emissions package because that state had passed emissions limits even more restrictive than California's. One thing could certainly be said about the Camaro—it was getting very expensive to buy and insure. Shades of the early 1970s! On the other hand, the fourth-generation Camaro ranked among the finest cars in the world in its price range. Chevrolet intended to keep it that way. Even more surprises awaited Camaro buyers in the remainder of the decade.

Chevy touted the high-tech tools it used for quality control. The ad also trumpeted the car's 275 horsepower, six-speed transmission, and 3-year/36,000-mile warranty. Chevrolet

SS—THE PERFECT BEAST IS BUILT

1 9 9 6 – 2 0 0 0

I n the early 1960s, Chevrolet introduced the SS moniker on a number of its cars. The Impala SS, Nova SS, and Chevelle SS were dressier versions of the standard line of cars with higher levels of interior and exterior trim. The Super Sports did not automatically come with the hottest engine that could be shoe-horned into the engine compartment. In fact, they typically were equipped with the standard engine of the base model. More go cost, more dough.

Naturally, when the Camaro was introduced for 1967, Chevrolet was there with an SS version: the Camaro SS350. Later the SS396 was added to the line. The big-block V-8 really made the Camaro a Super Sport. The Camaro SS thrived in the late 1960s, peaked in 1970, and began a downward slide burdened by emissions controls and sky-high insurance premiums. The Camaro SS ended not with a bang but with a whimper in 1972, powered by the 240-horsepower LS3 396 V-8 (actually 402 cubic inches). During the next two decades, the Z28

The 2000 SS was perhaps the greatest musclecar of its time. With 320 horsepower under the hood, it could run 0 to 60 miles per hour in 5.5 seconds and cover the quarter mile in 13.9 seconds. **David Newhardt**

In 1996 Chevrolet also brought back the Camaro RS. It included the exterior "cladding package," 200-horsepower 3.8-liter V-6, 16-inch wheels, and other features. It could be ordered as a coupe or convertible. **Chevrolet**

carried the performance torch and the once-great Camaro SS was forgotten.

The Camaro SS Returns

Some young automotive engineers remembered the Camaro SS and the performance it once represented. One of those men was Ed Hamburger. In 1987 he formed SLP (Street Legal Performance)

Engineering, Inc. Using his contacts at General Motors, Hamburger was able to convince Pontiac Division to sell SLP-modified Firebirds beginning in 1991. These cars were called Firehawks, having a higher level of performance and handling than even the Trans Am. SLP Engineering turned out only six cars in 1991, as the word of these special cars was slow to get out. The following year, a total of 19 were sold. Then things began to pick up: 201 Firehawks were sold in 1993, then 500 in 1994. Sales continued to climb and over 700 were sold in 1995.

Hamburger believed in his niche market and felt the Camaro could also benefit from the SLP treatment. He convinced Chevrolet to offer a truly higher performance Camaro, distinct from the Z28. COPO cars and specialty cars, like Yenko, Baldwin-Motion, and Berger Camaros, continue to be held in high esteem. Hamburger pitched a Camaro SS with a modified small-block V-8 with even more power than the engine in the Z28, special wheels and tires, functional high-performance hood, special rear spoiler, modified suspension, and other modifications. Chevrolet agreed and the Camaro SS project was launched.

Camaro. The 200-hp 3800 V6 is standard. So are the reviews.

"The best performance value in America now comes standard with the 3800 V6... which should put it right on top of the Mustang GT V8's acceleration figures." — *Motor Trend*

"Acceleration is vastly improved by every measure." — *Car and Driver*

"It's quiet and smooth, with tons of low-end torque and a satisfying feel when you run to the 6000 rpm redline." — *Motor Magazine*

"Quarter-mile and 0-60-mph times are more than a second quicker than before." — *Popular Mechanics*

Now that you know how the experts feel about the 3800 V6, test drive the Camaro and see for yourself. We're sure you'll agree it's as good as it looks on paper.

CAMARO 〜 GENUINE CHEVROLET

When Chevy released the stunning 200-horsepower, 3.8-liter V-6 in 1996, it let some of the magazines do the taking. The V-6 produced as much power as some V-8s on the market. **Chevrolet**

Using the same formula it had developed for the Firehawk, SLP gave the Camaro SS improved induction and exhaust flow to raise the output of the small-block LT1 V-8 from 285 horsepower to 305 horsepower. Wheels and tires developed for the ZR-1 Corvette were also part of the package, using 17x9-inch five-spoke wheels and P275-40-ZR17 tires. SLP did further suspension development, resulting in even stiffer front and rear suspension components.

But above all, it was the SLP-developed forced-air hood scoop that drew the attention of everyone on the road—including state police. Cold air hood induction had not been seen on the SS since 1969 with its famous "Super Scoop"—actually a reverse-facing scoop fed by high-pressure air at the base of the windshield. The SLP-designed hood scoop, using classic National Advisory Committee for Aeronautics (NACA) lines, drew cold, outside air into the massaged LT1. It was also an unmistakable performance styling statement that made the Camaro SS stand out on the road.

At the other end of the SS was an SLP-designed spoiler with slightly turned-up trailing edge. To ensure that everyone knew what they were staring at, SS badging appeared on the front fenders and rear bumper facia. Popping the hood of the SS revealed the air filter housing that received the incoming cold air. On the housing there was Z28 SS identification.

The SS Camaro was for those with deep pockets, those Young Urban (or suburban) Professionals in their 40s who grew up admiring the Camaro SS of the late 1960s as children and wanted their dose of performance now in the 1990s. The option code for the SS package was R7T and could only be ordered on the Z28. The base list price of the 1996 Z28 was $19,390. The SS option cost $3,999. Without tax, tag, title, or any other options, the Camaro SS set the buyer back nearly $25,000. While the customer waited for delivery, the order was sent to Chevrolet, which shipped a Z28 with the color and options desired to SLP in Michigan. SLP modified the car to specification, and then shipped the car back to Chevrolet for delivery to the dealer who ordered the car. The Camaro SS was an immediate sales success, with 2,410 sold in its first year.

There was a new performance kid on the block, and naturally the editors at every automotive magazine wanted to get their hands on the Camaro SS and

Chevrolet brought back the Camaro SS in 1996. The SS begins life as a Z28 and is modified by SLP at its Canadian facility near the Camaro assembly plant. The niche market of the SS has proved very successful. SLP Engineering

Chevrolet built the GM Performance Parts F1 Specialty Vehicle to show existing Camaro owners they could advance the looks, handling and performance of their cars. The parts could be ordered individually or as a complete package. Chevrolet

Chevrolet celebrated the Camaro's 30th anniversary in 1997 with an anniversary edition available on the Z28 Coupe or Convertible. You could have any color, as long as it was Arctic White with Hugger Orange stripes. **Chevrolet**

For 1998, Chevrolet gave the fourth-generation Camaro a facelift. The SS naturally benefited from the change, and SLP designed a new performance hood in response. Sales of the SS continued to climb. Jerry Ormand

give their impressions of the car. Even the automotive consumer buyer's guides published by Edmund Publications got hold of a flaming red Camaro SS. The editors experienced what maximum performance and attention could do to the driver. The SS, they stated, was not for every prospective Camaro buyer:

"The Z28 is not an ordinary car to begin with, because it is much faster than anything else on the road for the money. Check the SS option package box on the order sheet and you'll be rewarded with a forced-air-induction, tire-smoking menace to society. We want to state very clearly that this option package should only be chosen by those who really like to go fast all of the time. It is not meant for the weekend warrior who would need to drive the car sedately five days out of the week, and it is most certainly not meant for people who would never need to drive the car in inclement weather.

"The Z28 SS isn't like other cars; driving it is a lot of work. We had a great time taking it through our road courses, and were amazed by the car's rock-solid stability and faultless antilock brakes, but the jarring suspension setup makes the car jumpy on all but the smoothest of roads, causing constant correction by the driver. The big Z-rated tires are on a virtual quest to remove drivers from their intended course by following any truck rut or pavement irregularity into oblivion. Differentiating the SS from lesser Camaros is easy. The poodle-swallowing hood scoop, giant tires, and distinct badges let every state trooper in the county know that you are a speed freak. The booming exhaust will annoy your neighbors, and the snarling engine burble will cause parents to clutch their children protectively when you cruise down the road."

No question about it; the Camaro SS was perfectly executed. After the bleak, desperate years of the 1970s and 1980s, the Camaro SS returned in uncompromising form and able to compete on the road with some of the highest performance and most expensive cars on the road. Who would have thought that one day Chevrolet would sell a street Camaro capable of 160 miles per hour?

Refining the Legend

For most Camaro buyers looking for performance, the Z28 more than satisfied the need for speed. Output of the LT1 V-8 had been bumped up by 10 horsepower to 285 as a result of Chevrolet's

Will the Camaro drive into the automotive sunset? If so, the Z28 Convertible will no doubt rank among the instant collectable cars of the new millennium. Camaro enthusiasts with their eyes on the future are buying them now. Chevrolet

The Camaro for 2000 remained one of the world's finest cars in its class. With its standard 200-horsepower V-6, four-wheel disc brakes, and superb balance and handling, it is also one of the most enjoyable cars to drive. Chevrolet

137

CAMARO ENVY

For years the Camaro has meant a great deal to owners of the car, but what one rarely reads about is what others think of the Camaro. The automotive editors at Edmund's Publications pondered on this after extensively road testing a 1996 Z28 SS. It is an insightful examination of what goes on in the minds of other drivers when encountering Chevrolet's alpha-numeric musclecar.

"Why are we so quick to judge drivers of Camaros? Is it because they drive poorly? No, Camaro drivers typically pilot their cars as well as the rest of the road-going populace. Is it because they blast obnoxious music out of their vehicles? Although this is sometimes the case, it is certainly not the norm . . .. They must be doing something to warrant all of this negative attention. We think that it is because Camaro drivers drive fast, and as we all know from high school driver's education classes, speed kills. Not only do Camaro drivers exceed the speed limit, they usually do it [in] such a way that makes the non-Camaro driving population look silly. By accelerating quickly away from a stoplight, Camaros can safely maneuver for the best lane position when traffic is heavy. With plenty of torque everywhere in the powerband, Camaro drivers can cleave through freeway traffic like a hot knife through butter. In other words, by stomping on the long, skinny pedal, Camaro drivers can exit the sad, slow world of minivan madness and sedan sluggishness.

"This makes minivan and sedan drivers green with envy, and in retaliation, they try and slow the Camaro's pace; often performing amazingly stupid acts to make sure the Camaro doesn't get ahead of them. We at Edmund's think that it is a psychological thing. People don't want to be passed, because in some strange Darwinian manner, speed implies power and success. Thus by bottlenecking traffic in a Lincoln Continental or Dodge Caravan, drivers can assure themselves that they are, in fact, swift and powerful, when in reality they are merely the crippled mountain goat ready to be downed by the lurking cougar.

"Nowhere, it seems, is this psychological dysfunction more apparent than the streets of Denver, Colorado. The fear of being passed is so great here that drivers will not move out of the left lane of traffic even if they are going 10 mph under the posted speed limit with a horde of fast movers descending on them like locusts. Witness the experience of our managing editor in the Camaro SS. While serenely driving down C-470, a

SLP modifications to produce the SS include installing functional ram air hood and intake, unique rear spoiler, improved exhaust system, unique wheels and tires, and other modifications that make it the most powerful and best-handling Camaro ever built.
SLP Engineering

big looping stretch of freeway that circles the south and west parts of Denver, Chris came upon a minivan slowly cruising in the left lane. Our test Z28 SS was bright red and equipped with GM's ever-present daytime running lights. We are certain that only the certifiably blind could have missed the car. Chris hung respectfully behind the minivan for a minute or two, waiting for the driver to notice him and move over. Since this was Denver, Chris' politeness was sorely wasted. The minivan failed to yield to the faster-moving traffic, forcing Chris to attempt to pass on the right. When Chris moved into the right lane, the minivan moved over too; straddling the center line, leaving no room to pass on the left or right. Chris, who has much more patience than this editor, moved back to the left lane, thinking that perhaps the minivan was trying to move right to let him by. No such luck. Once that minivan had Chris and the pesky Z28 SS back in the left lane, he too moved back into the left lane. This process was repeated a number of times, with Chris' blood pressure slowly rising, until a third lane opened up, at which point Chris dropped the hammer and flew past the idiotic minivan. The minivanner, noticeably chagrined at having his masculinity unsurped by the threatening, shark-toothed Camaro, immediately sped up and rode Chris's rear bumper. Ironically, the traffic ahead of Chris slowed quickly, causing Chris to come to an abrupt stop. The driver of the minivan wasn't paying attention, great idea when you're tailgating, and failed to notice until the last moment that the traffic in front of him was no longer moving. He had to jam on the brakes, and according to Chris, spilled coffee all over himself in the process. Final score? Camaro 1, Minivan 0.

"My guess is that this is the real reason people hate Camaros. Camaros are aggressive-looking cars that are often owned by aggressive drivers. Drivers that are not likely to suffer fools or left-lane bandits kindly. As a result, when someone tries to hold a Camaro up, they are likely to be embarrassed. Nobody likes to be embarrassed, so the resulting animosity towards Camaros grows at each occurrence. If you are suffering from this Camarophobia, we can offer a simple solution: go out and buy a Camaro. You don't necessarily need a Z28 SS; the less exotic varieties will suffice, and your fears of being passed will be alleviated. Not many vehicles are faster than a Chevy Camaro to begin with, and for the price, there is nothing that's an even match."

upgraded On-Board Diagnostic system using two catalytic converters for a true dual exhaust system, and the use of an oxygen sensor for each exhaust bank. This was the biggest news for the 1996 Z28. There were only subtle changes aside from this, with new interior and exterior colors and interior fabrics. The base list price of the Z28 reflected the technological refinements and changes to the exhaust system, leaping nearly $1,500 to $19,390. The Z28 Convertible was the most expensive of the Camaro line, with a base sticker of $24,490.

Such price rises, however, were not caused just by the cost of new technology, but the rising prices of the vendor-supplied components to Chevrolet. In fact, the true rate of inflation in America could accurately be tracked using the Manufacturer's Suggested Retail Price (MSRP) from one year to the next. The "Camaro Price Index" is a truer indicator of inflation. However, the price of the Camaro in the 1990s also reflected how dramatically the car had improved over the years in terms of power, emissions, handling, and safety.

The Rally Sport Returns

Chevrolet added two new models to the Camaro line for 1996. The Rally Sport Coupe and the Rally Sport Convertible were positioned between the Camaro Coupe and Convertible, and the Z28 Coupe and Convertible. The main distinction of the RS was its appearance, based on what Chevrolet called a Cladding Package. In this package were front and rear facia extensions, rocker moldings, three-piece rear spoiler, and black RS emblem on the front fenders and rear facia. There was other equipment that came standard on the RS. This included air conditioning and handsome 16-inch aluminum wheels fitted with P235/55R tires. The RS Coupe was roughly $2,500 higher than the base Coupe, which listed for $14,995. Over 8,000 buyers chose the RS Coupe in 1996, but just 905 purchased the RS Convertible, perhaps due to the $22,720 price tag.

Steady as She Goes

Virtually no changes took place on the outside of the Camaro Coupe and Convertible. If you popped the hood, however, there was big news—a new, larger displacement V-6. The 3.8-liter L36 V-6 pumped out 200 horsepower. This equated to 52.6 horsepower per liter, compared to the 50 horsepower per liter for the LT1. This engine came standard in the Camaro Coupe and Convertible and RS Coupe and Convertible. The boost in power and torque also resulted in a boost in price, nearly $750 on the Coupe. These rapidly rising prices on all Camaros finally had an impact on sales. Overall Camaro

The 2000 Camaro SS featured a well appointed interior. An easy-to-read analog speedometer and tachometer lets the driver know exactly how the car is performing. The four-spoke steering wheel has stereo controls, so the driver never had to take a hand off the wheel to find the right music. David Newhardt

sales were cut in half to 61,362 from the previous year's 122,738. Technology had accomplished many things for the Camaro, but technology had not succeeded in holding the line on inflation, let alone lowering the price.

The Camaro's once mysterious special performance packages had become mainstream. The 1LE option was consolidated with the other options necessary to trigger the desired performance equipment and now listed for $1,175; a total of 55 were sold in 1996. The B4C Special Service Package continued to find acceptance with police departments as the F16 equivalent to a police interceptor; 225 were sold in 1996.

In 1997, Chevrolet celebrated 30 years of Camaro production, naturally offering a 30th Anniversary Edition. The option was available only on the Z28 Coupe and Convertible and listed for $575. It included an Arctic White exterior with Hugger Orange hood and trunk stripes and exterior identification. The Coupe roof was a matching Arctic White. Five-spoke aluminum wheels were also painted white and mounted with P245 tires. The interior featured seating surfaces of optional white leather or standard

The all-aluminum LS1 is the most powerful 350-ci production V-8 Chevrolet has ever built. It gained fame powering the Corvette, and it is appropriately housed in the Camaro SS. A fiberglass cold-air hood scoop and dual exhaust allow the car to breathe. David Newhardt

white leather with cloth houndstooth inserts. The all-leather interior came with the 30th Anniversary logo stamped on the headrest, while the leather and cloth interior featured a stitched logo on the headrest. Special anniversary embroidery also appeared on the floormats. All 1997 Camaros received the 30th Anniversary embossed headrests.

There was a new interior in the Camaro for 1997, with new instrument panel, seat design, and console with numerous useful features. The seats were improved with greater lumbar support. A CD player had been an option in the Camaro for several years, and in 1997 this option was expanded to offer a 12-disc remote CD changer.

Overall sales of the Camaro dropped again in 1997, to just over 55,000 units. But a bright spot was the Camaro SS. Sales jumped over 1,000 cars from the previous year to 3,430 units. The price remained unchanged from its inaugural year and so did its reputation as one of the fastest and best-handling cars in the world under $30,000.

The Z28 Convertible remained the most expensive model in the Camaro line and for 1997 had a list price of $25,520. The Z28 Coupe followed at $20,115. Sticker shock was taking its toll on prospective Camaro buyers. The base Camaro Coupe model now had an MSRP of $16,215, but air conditioning was now standard on all Camaro models. The Camaro Convertible now cost $21,770. The RS Coupe and Convertible split the price differential.

A New Face and a New Heart

Chevrolet had not been neglecting the Camaro's appearance or its motive power. For 1998 the Camaro sported a completely new front end, with redesigned hood, fenders, facia, and headlight design. Underneath there was a revised four-wheel disc brake system, now standard on all Camaro models. Coupled with the standard antilock braking system (ABS), the 1998 Camaro was the safest Camaro ever built. The Camaro now featured a new one-piece, all-welded exhaust system designed to reduce noise and vibration. The RS Coupe and Convertible were dropped from the Camaro line for 1998. Buyers could choose from the Camaro Coupe, Convertible, Z28 Coupe, and Z28 Convertible. And, of course, there was the SS option.

The front fascia of the SS has evolved since it was introduced in 1996. The dual halogen headlights and driving lights provide superb illumination during nighttime driving duties. David Newhardt

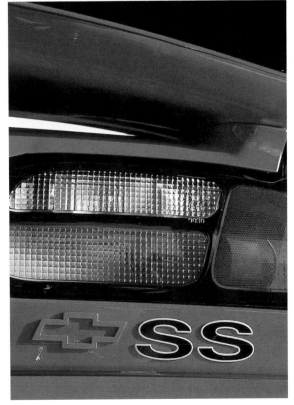

The graphic identifies the car as the top-of-the-line Camaro. The SS' solid rear axle suspension provides excellent road holding characteristics. This modern musclecar is fitted with Goodyear F1 GS radials on 17-inch wheels. David Newhardt.

The cast-aluminum wheels on the 2000 SS were new and were the largest wheels ever fitted to a Camaro. David Newhardt

The really big news for 1998 was the new generation small-block V-8 under the hood of the Z28. GM Powertrain had taken the venerable 350-ci V-8 to its next evolution with the LS1—an all-aluminum V-8 that drastically cut the V-8 engine's weight and improved the level of horsepower even further. The new intake manifold was made of composite material and had superior flow characteristics to the LT1. This new V-8, introduced first in the Corvette, had a slightly lower rating in the Camaro due to a different camshaft grind and exhaust system so it would not embarrass the Corvette. In Z28 tune, the LS1 generated 305 horsepower and 335 ft-lb of torque. This engine also featured a new drive-by-wire electronic throttle.

Of course, the top of the Camaro performance pyramid was the SS option on the Z28. In the SS the LS1 developed 320 horsepower at 5,200 rpm with 345 ft-lb of torque at 4,000 rpm. *Road & Track* got around to testing a Camaro SS in 1998, but it prefaced its road test with bad news. Editor Andrew Bornhop wrote, "Hard to believe, but this is possibly the last Camaro road test we'll ever write. After 31 years of production, General Motors is on the brink of dropping both the Chevy Camaro and its F-body brother, the Pontiac Firebird. Say it ain't so! We wish

we could, but lagging sales are to blame." Unfortunately, Bornhop offered no substantiation but referred only to another article in that issue. This article did much to fuel fears of the Camaro's imminent demise. Editorial armchair prognosticators issued similar rhetoric, but never quoted individuals at GM or Chevrolet saying production of the Camaro would cease.

After giving the bad news, *Road & Track* proceeded to say, "Camaro fans have an ally in the 1998 SS, the best argument yet to keep the Camaro alive." Acceleration was half the game with the Camaro SS. The editors wrote the SS reached 60 miles per hour in 5.5 seconds and blitzed the quarter-mile in 13.9 seconds at 105.7 miles per hour. The elapsed time would have been lower, but the amazing power and torque of the LS1 made it difficult for the tires to keep hold of the asphalt during initial acceleration. Hauling the SS to a stop was undramatic, thanks to its four huge disc brakes, which were assisted by a new Bosch ABS. The SS came to a stop from 60 miles per hour in only 129 feet, and from 80 miles per hour in 222 feet. It had the most impressive handling of any Camaro the editors had ever driven. In closing, the magazine wrote: "So, this latest Camaro SS is quick, tight, remarkably civil and boatloads of fun. It's the least expensive 320 bhp money can buy. And for $27,640 as equipped, it's a poor man's Corvette."

Road & Track was right about one thing. Production continued to decline and for 1998, a total of 54,020 Camaros were built. Numbers for 1LE cars doubled from 1997 to 99 units. Production of the SS dipped 12 percent to 3,017 cars.

For the last year of the millennium, the 1999 Camaro line continued virtually unchanged, having just come off a year of significant changes both outside and under the hood. The year, in fact, continued along undramatically until November. On November 12th, it was leaked to the media that GM would indeed halt production of the Firebird and Camaro in the near future.

Thunderstruck Camaro enthusiasts raced to the Internet to find out anything they could. CNN's financial Web page announced, "GM drops Camaro, Firebird. Top U.S. carmaker will stop building both models next year. General Motors Corp. plans to stop making the Chevrolet Camaro and Pontiac Firebird models next year, a published report said Friday.

"The Camaro and Firebird and the Trans Am version of the Firebird will be dropped from GM's product line-up in 2000, a senior GM official told the *Oakland Press* of Pontiac.

" 'I'm not going to kid you; the nameplates are going to go away for a while,' said the official, who asked not to be identified. 'The nameplates could resurface on new products in the future, but the company's plans are indefinite,' he said.

"Speculation about the future of both cars intensified last month after Canadian Auto Workers union president Buzz Hargrove disclosed that GM planned to close its assembly plant in Ste. Therese, Quebec, where the cars are made, by fall 2000.

"Hargrove was unable to persuade GM to keep the plant open beyond next fall, but GM officials have declined to discuss the fate of the cars publicly. Camaros and Firebirds have been an integral part of the GM model line-up since the late 1960s, when they first appeared to compete with the popular Ford Mustang.

"Combined sales have dropped to less than half of the 150,000 units GM officials had thought they could sell when current models were planned in the early 1990s, the newspaper said."

Chevrolet was quick to respond. The same day as the CNN announcement, the GM division issued the following press release:

General Motors Corp. Statement Regarding Future Plans for the Chevrolet Camaro and Pontiac Firebird

While as a policy General Motors Corp. does not publicly discuss its long-term future product plans, recent reports of the Chevrolet Camaro and Pontiac Firebird's pending demise are inaccurate. GM has stated previously that the company is committed to continue operation of the Ste. Therese, Quebec, plant through the term of the current Canadian Auto Workers contract that expires

This bird's eye view shows the distinctive body style of the Camaro SS with its elongated hood and the large rear window glass. David Newhardt

The SLP-designed forced-air hood scoop is one of most distinguishing features on the new SS Camaros. This functional hood scoop drew cold outside air and stuffed it into the intake of the 305-horsepower LT1. David Newhardt

The SS was reintroduced in 1996 to the rave reviews of the press. Performance was widely praised but the styling package was impressive as well. The rear spoiler is distinctive and tasteful. David Newhardt

in fall 2002. At this time, no product has been assigned to the plant after that date, but GM continues to study possible options. Nothing has changed concerning GM's production plans for the Camaro and Firebird. In fact, special editions of the Camaro and Firebird are in development for the 2002 model year.

The press release was very carefully worded, but here at last was the fact of the matter from General Motors Corp. itself. Following the production cycle for each generation Camaro of roughly 10 years, the fifth generation Camaro should appear in 2003. Now, however, there would be no Camaro production at all after 2002. To judge from the remarks by the nameless GM executive, the *nameplate* might eventually be applied to other products, meaning a Camaro name on some other type of Chevrolet car. That move has always spelled doom in the marketplace, however, because car buyers are no fools. And, there are precedents in Chevrolet's own history. The Monte Carlo ceased production in 1988 after nearly two decades, and no violins were heard when the last one rolled down the assembly line. The nameplate appeared some years later on a front-wheel drive car, but the old Monte Carlo fans didn't line up to buy one.

There are numerous other Chevrolet models that were introduced, sold for a number of years, then vanished from the Chevrolet line. The purpose of General Motors is to build cars, make a profit, and pay dividends to stockholders. The continued dramatic rise in the Camaro's price in the 1990s contributed to its declining sales and everything indicated this trend would continue. It was hard to conceive life in America could go on without this automotive icon, but some automotive editors were not totally surprised by the fact or against the idea of stopping production of the Camaro. GM had economic realities to consider, not buyer sentimentality.

On December 31, 1999, tens of millions of people around the world stayed up for a very special New Year's Eve. Many were celebrating the beginning of a new millennium, but in the back of everyone's mind was the Y2K bug. Businesses and governments grappled with the problem of making sure computers successfully read the rollover from '99' to '00' in billions of lines of computer code and in operating systems, programs, and data bases around the world. When midnight in each time zone came and went with no apparent computer glitches or power blackouts, planes did not fall from the sky, and ATMs dispensed money without problems, it was a testament to thousands of people who worked to make sure the advent of the New Millennium was a nonevent. Life would go on as before, but there would be changes. The days of the Camaro were growing short.

If everyone owned one, maybe we could have prevented disco.

Camaro Z28.
Disco. It was a pimple on the face of music history. And while polyester suits had their 15 minutes of fame, Rock 'n Roll is here to stay. So is the Chevy™ Camaro Z28? With eight cylinders and 285 horses, it's the only way to boogie.

Genuine Chevrolet
The Cars More Americans Trust.

Few cars can boast a history that pre-dates the disco era of the 1970s. The fourth generation 1997 Camaro was one of the few. With 285 horsepower under the hood, the Z28 left no doubt American automotive high-performance was alive and well in the late 1990s. **Chevrolet**

The 2000 Camaro had already been in dealers' showrooms for several months and there were new features to lure prospective buyers. A new convenience feature inside the Camaro included redundant radio controls on the steering wheel, so drivers could change the music without taking their eyes from the road. While the annual model change had disappeared back in the late 1960s, it was still routine to offer new exterior colors and interior fabrics. That tradition continued with the 2000 Camaro.

Chevrolet' superb LS1 V-8 had been voted one of the "10 Best Engines" in the world by *Ward's Auto World,* a respected industry journal, for the last three years and it snagged the award again in 2000. There were improvements to the LS1 for 2000. The engine block was revised, there were new close-coupled catalytic converters, a new progressive throttle cam, replacing the previous linear design, a new engine rear cover, new cast-iron exhaust manifolds, improved emissions air pump, a new starter motor, and other refinements.

Outside, the only notable change was the adoption of matching-color outside mirrors and a new cast-aluminum wheel design for the Z28 and SS. The spirit of performance remained alive in the Camaro and was prominently displayed in the 2000 brochure. The brochure featured a bright red Z28 at speed filling both pages, with the headline, "Are You Ready for a 6-speed, 305-HP Ride?" The two pages also quoted the accolades heaped upon the Z28 by *Car & Driver, Automobile Magazine,* and *Sports Car Illustrated.* On the next two pages was an Arctic White Z28 Convertible and above it this unabashed statement: "Z28. Thirty-Three Years of Total Domination."

That really sums up the life of the Camaro ever since it was introduced in the fall of 1966. The Camaro survived the insurance lobby, the emissions era, the bumper era, recessions, and countless competitors to become one of the longest running and most popular cars in the history of the automobile. It will forever remain in the hearts of all who have owned and driven one.

CHAPTER 10

CAMARO RACING WORLD WIDE

1967 – 2000

Perhaps no activity has more impact on an automobile than racing. As long as cars have existed, people have raced them. In the days when stock cars were truly stock, production cars had a high attrition rate. It was a simple case of survival of the strongest. Sometimes the most insignificant part would fail and knock a car out of the race. As time went on during the 1960s and 1970s, racing cars came to bear no resemblance to stock. This was true of NASCAR. NHRA and AHRA had modified classes of various levels. The SCCA is, perhaps, the one sanctioning body that endeavored to promote racing of cars as close to stock configuration as possible.

In the mid-1960s, the SCCA introduced a racing series for two-door sedans—the Trans-American series, or Trans-Am for short. Ford pursued this series with its Mustang and dominated the 1965 season.

As the Camaro was nearing production, Vince Piggins proposed to Chevrolet general manager Pete

Chevrolet built the ZL1 Camaro in 1969, and made it available only as COPO 9560. The all-aluminum 427 had its roots in Can-Am development and used numerous parts from the race-proven iron-block L88. The ZL1's breathing was grossly restricted with the factory exhaust system, which was immediately discarded for tube headers and a custom exhaust system before it headed for the drag strip. Mike Mueller

147

The production Z28, conceived and built to compete in the SCCA Trans-Am series, was the basis of such cars as Roger Penske's No. 6, driven with consummate skill by Mark Donohue. Here, Donohue is shown during the 1967 season.

Estes a special Camaro configured to compete in Trans-Am races at the hands of independent teams. Piggins emphasized *independent* teams because GM had a very strict edict regarding factory racing. That edict was, basically, no direct factory racing. Chevrolet's previous general manager, Semon "Bunkie" Knudsen, had been called on the carpet by the GM board of directors when it was found out the 427-ci "Mystery Motor" raced at Daytona was, in fact, a racing engine developed behind closed doors at Chevrolet. The engine wasn't production at all—as required by NASCAR rules. When the Ford people suspected this at trackside, they filed a complaint with NASCAR officials. In order to compete at the Daytona 500, the

Chevrolet personnel at Daytona were forced to sell two of the engines to Ford to "prove" it was a production engine! When news of this got back to the GM building, Knudsen was summoned to give an explanation. Heads almost rolled over this breach of corporate policy, but the fallout was eventual production of this new engine design for Chevrolet passenger cars and trucks in 396- and 427-ci displacements.

With this event still in his mind, Piggins wanted to avoid all appearance of impropriety. He wanted to offer a Camaro within the five-liter (305 cubic inches) displacement limit to compete in Trans-Am, and develop the production car totally above board. The goal was to build a car on the production line that was driveable on the street, but strong enough to hand over to racers for them to massage and take racing.

Estes felt the division would be walking a fine line, but he agreed with Piggins' idea, stating that Chevrolet would lose sales if it didn't offer a Camaro to compete with the Mustang and other makes. The SCCA rules for Trans-Am were patterned after the European FIA rules: basically, 1,000 units of the car with modifications had to be built and sold. For Chevrolet, that would not be difficult to do.

To meet the 5.0-liter displacement limit, Piggins had to do some parts swapping. The 283 was too small and the 327 too large. The 283 had a 3.87-inch bore with a 3.00-inch stroke. The 327 had a 4.00-inch bore with a 3.25-inch stroke. However, both engines shared the same main bearing dimensions. Piggins ran the numbers and found a 283 crankshaft in the

The big-block Camaro also became the choice of Chevy racers on the quarter-mile. This SS396 waits for its opponent at California's famed Irwindale Raceway in 1968.

327 block resulted in a 302-ci V-8. The 4.00-inch bore with 3.00-inch stroke would make the engine perfect in the high rpm racing environment.

However, to go racing, the guts of the new 302 V-8 had to be designed to develop the power needed, survive the grueling racing environment—and be sold in the car to be driven on the street. This would be a new high-performance small-block V-8, and would undergo the same rigorous engine development as any other at Chevrolet.

Piggins relished the engineering project for both the engine and the car, and Don McPherson's engine group went to work. Development of this engine and the Z28 itself is recorded in chapter 1. Many of the high performance pieces were already on hand, and Piggins and McPherson knew what had to be done to make the engine and vehicle survive. The certification of the parts and homologation of the vehicle moved very quickly. By the end of November, two months after the rollout of the Camaro, a new model was on display at Riverside Raceway the weekend of the race there. A fact sheet listed the vehicle as the Z28, the RPO for the long list of high-performance equipment installed on the car. The more questions were asked, the more the answers indicated this Camaro could indeed go racing. Chevrolet representatives hastened to point out, however, that Chevrolet itself was not going to race it. The automotive press was quick to stir the pot, and Chevrolet was just as quick to quell the rumors. It was all grand showmanship really, and worked to generate interest among just those amateur and professional racers and teams to whom Chevrolet wanted to sell the car.

One of those very interested parties was Roger Penske, a prosperous Chevrolet dealer, a former winning race driver himself, and a team manager. The Z28 really had his attention. Penske made an appointment with Estes, and brought the big guns with him: representatives from SUNOCO, who would sponsor Penske's racing effort—if Chevrolet would support its product.

Estes told them the Z28 formed an excellent base from which they could go racing, with allowable modifications within SCCA rules. He agreed with Penske's pitch that the Trans-Am was the Z28's best venue. Estes said the division could not advertise the wins to promote either the Z28 or the teams that

raced it. However, the division would offer product support in the form of advice from the ride and handling engineering groups, and the small high-performance engine group. Of course, Chevrolet would be glad to sell them the latest parts developed for the car. Certainly, parts that failed under the rigors of racing would have to be reengineered and brought to production as quickly as possible. Estes assured them this would be done, as part of ongoing product improvement. Penske and the SUNOCO reps got what they wanted. But Estes was smiling too, because Chevrolet's newest model, the Z28, was going to get some first-class exposure, and the division didn't have to spend a dime in advertising to do it.

Piggins was not the only one within Chevrolet looking at the racing potential of the Camaro. Piggins reported to Walter Burwell, who wanted to expand the areas of racing for the Camaro. Alex Mair, Chevrolet's director of engineering, received a memo from Burwell giving a detailed description of the different classes of racing the Camaro could compete in, including drag racing and sports car racing. The company would have to develop improved powerplants and suspension designs to ensure racers had the strongest and most reliable Camaro Chevrolet could provide.

The cars as delivered still needed work in order to be raced safely. Certain heavy-duty racing parts could be installed on the car after it left the factory, replacing parts likely to break and put the vehicle

The heart of the Z28 was its 302 V-8, engineered to withstand the grueling Trans-Am environment. This factory photo shows the 52x4-barrel cross-ram-induction system and the racing headers Chevrolet engineered for the 302. Note the four-bolt main bearing caps on the engine block.

The Trans-Am 302 with cross-ram-induction system photographed in one of Chevrolet's test cells at the Engineering Center. The photo was taken sometime in 1968. The engine developed roughly 400 horsepower on the dyno.

The team of Penske and Donohue had its best Trans-Am season in 1969. After two seasons of getting the Z28 sorted out, Donohue took home the Championship in 1969. Here Donohue is shown at Laguna Seca. **Bob Tronolone**

ishes, the Penske team won its first Trans-Am race at Marboro, Maryland, in the middle of the season. The team won the last two events of 1967, a harbinger of the 1968 season.

The Penske team now had the car properly set up, as proved by 10 wins in the 12 Trans-Am races held in 1968. Donohue won 8 straight. The Penske team took the championship that year. In 1969, Donohue battled with Parnelli Jones in his Mustang practically the entire season; Donohue won 6 of the final 7 races, and the championship. For 1970, however, Penske made the unlikely decision to switch to American Motors Corporation and race its Javelin. Jim Hall and Team Chaparral took Penske's place. Owens Corning backed Tony DeLorenzo and Jerry Thompson; they had raced Corvettes the previous year. However, the larger ports and valves of the Boss 302 gave the Mustang superior power, with 40 to 50 more horsepower than the Z28. Ford won the 1970 Trans-Am championship with 72 points, AMC with Penske and Donohue scored 59 points, and Chevrolet finished third with 40 points. Ford, Dodge, and Plymouth all dropped out of Trans-Am racing at the end of the season and so did Chevrolet.

The ZL-1 Camaro

One of the hottest areas of auto racing in the late 1960s was Can-Am. Jim Hall and Bruce McLaren raced the small-block V-8 in their race cars, but this engine was short on torque. The iron-block 427

or driver at risk. These included front spindles, axles, and related bushings. In addition, a larger capacity fuel tank could be installed.

The first 24-hour event the Penske Camaro entered was the 24 Hours of Daytona. Mark Donohue had raced No. 6 in the Daytona Trans-Am event but dropped out with valvetrain problems. Penske chose to fix the car and wait for the 24-hour event. The car suffered mechanical problems during this race also, but not before repeatedly clocking over 160 miles per hour down the Daytona back straight.

As the most visible team campaigning the Z28, the Penske team spent the first half of 1967 sorting the car and working with Piggins to make it bulletproof. An aggressive program of heavy-duty parts development was in full swing. Piggins was a very busy man. After many disappointments and low-place fin-

Chevrolet dealer Fred Gibb took delivery of the first ZL1 Camaro built, and the car was campaigned extensively. After years of racing, Gibb sold the car and it went through several owners. Bill Porterfield, a ZL1 owner, saw an ad for the car and bought it. An extensive and expensive restoration followed. This car is rolling automotive history, and is still raced today. **Jack Underwood**

introduced in 1966 held promise for real power generation, but it was significantly heavier than the small-block. Bill Howell was a development engineer whose second home was the row of dynamometer cells at the Chevrolet Engineering Center in Warren, Michigan. Howell was there during the glory days of big-block performance development.

"The aluminum block stuff came about as a result of the Chaparral R & D program when the Chaparral team decided that the small-block was no longer going to be viable against the McLarens and other competitors," Howell says. "They were running a two-speed automatic transmission, and that transmission needed a lot of torque. With only two gears, you need a broad power range. So, they decided to go to the big-block in aluminum with a built-in dry sump system. It was an iron-liner 427. They ran that as an exclusive with Chaparral for one year. McLaren was running the cast-iron small-block when the Chaparral was the aluminum big-block."

McLaren was at a distinct disadvantage and was about to switch to Ford engines when Piggins stepped in and convinced McLaren they could have the aluminum 427 too. Chevrolet made a run of those experimental castings and parts and sold them not only to McLaren, but also to anyone who wanted to run the aluminum 427 in 1968. McLaren took the engine and dominated the field with it in Can-Am.

"We then decided there was a market for an aluminum big-block racing engine, certainly in Can-Am racing and drag racing. Vince, more than anyone else, lobbied for an aluminum version of the 427 block," recalls Howell. "One of the smart things Vince always did was analyze something to find out whether we could compete with it in the first place, and if we couldn't, he wouldn't bother."

Funding to design and build a limited production racing aluminum 427 was approved. The task of managing the program fell to Zora Arkus-Duntov. Fred Frincke had worked on the Can-Am engine development and Arkus-Duntov selected him to be

When Penske switched from Chevrolet to AMC for the 1970 Trans-Am season, Jim Hall and Team Chaparral took up the Camaro banner. Bob Tronolone snapped Hall in No. 1, followed by Ed Leslie in No. 2 at Turn Number 9 at Leguna Seca in April 1970. Bob Tronolone

principal engineer. Although the ZL-1 shared dimensions with the 427-ci iron-block L88 racing engine, its aluminum construction required special considerations. Duntov and Frincke took into account aluminum's unique mechanical and thermal properties, and incorporated the features that racers desired. The block would be cast from 356 T-6 aluminum alloy and feature iron liners. Due to the weaker nature of aluminum, the block was beefed up and structurally reinforced in needed areas.

Except for the camshaft, the L88 and ZL-1 used the same rotating and reciprocating parts. The crankshaft was forged from SAE 5140 steel and Tufftrided. Connecting rods were stronger than the standard street 427 rods and used larger diameter bolts. The unique mechanical camshaft had timing similar to the 1969 L88 cam, but intake and exhaust lifts were greater for the ZL-1. Tom Langdon worked on

The ZL-1 427 aluminum big-block marked the apex of Mk IV V-8 high-performance development. Because Chevrolet installed the engine in production cars, the ZL-1 had to be fitted with complete emissions equipment with air injection pump and plumbing. Cast-iron exhaust manifolds were a production necessity and replaced with tube headers to unleash the engine's 500-plus horsepower. **GM Powertrain**

Gentlemen, start your Camaros.

The third annual International Race of Champions is on.

Once again, in four fascinating events spread widely across the country and the calendar, 12 of the world's winningest drivers are competing in 12 identical cars,

identically prepared. A true test of driving skill.

The cars are Camaros.

That should come as no great surprise. Camaro's aerodynamic shape makes it a natural for these events. The profile is low,

the stance is wide, the size is right—and the feel is terrific. Drivers enjoy driving Camaros, people enjoy watching them.

Camaro has been a particularly popular off-road competition car ever since it was first introduced about 10 years ago.

Chevrolet salutes the 12 distinguished drivers of the third International Race of Champions.

Gentlemen, start your Camaros. **Chevrolet**

WATCH FOR THE INTERNATIONAL RACE OF CHAMPIONS ON THE ABC TELEVISION NETWORK.

The International Race of Champions was a boon for the Camaro's image in the 1970s and 1980s. Here, the 12 drivers, minus one, pose behind Benny Parsons' No. 12 for this ad, which appeared in the January 1976 Hot Rod.

development of the L88 and ZL-1 and recalled this work on the aluminum 427.

"We were concerned about the durability of the valvetrain," says Langdon. "That had been a persistent limiting factor on the durability of the engine when operating in a race application, so we were very cognizant of the limitations of the relatively heavy valvetrain. We found a camshaft that evolved into the release camshaft for the 1969 ZL-1."

Durability testing's objective was to complete a 24-hour high-speed simulation of the 24 Hours of Daytona. A number of engines were run-in and power checked, then shipped out for installation in the DeLorenzo Corvette to be tested under actual racing conditions. This confirmed the ZL-1 power-making ability and durability, and limited production of the ZL-1 was approved.

Winters Foundry in Ohio was selected to cast the block, heads, and intake manifold. Raw aluminum castings were shipped to GM's Tonawanda, New York, engine plant to be machined before moving on to the assembly phase. Art Casper had worked as an industrial engineer at Tonawanda since 1964. He says the ZL-1 required procedures for machining and assembly that were different from iron-block engines.

"We set up a special, in-house shop," Casper says. "We bought an Omni-Mill, a programmable machine. By writing a computer program, it would select the proper tools and do progressive operations for you. We took the engine case from the raw casting and ended up with a finished product."

Casper and his small team developed a special means of inserting the iron liners by heating the block to permit installing the liners, then letting the block cool to capture them. A special clean room was set up for assembly of each ZL-1. It was air conditioned at a constant temperature. Each engine was blueprinted and took roughly 16 hours to build. The engine was serialized and taken out to the test

The Reher-Morrison team raced its second-generation Camaro in Pro Stock with great success. The team established a winning reputation for Chevrolet as great as that of Sox & Martin for Plymouth. Chevrolet

department where it was broken in for one hour. Then it was taken to the test lab and run in on a specific program there. The advertised horsepower was 430, but Casper remembers no ZL-1 generating less than 500 horsepower.

Fred Gibb, Chevrolet dealer in Illinois, drew up an agreement with the division to purchase 50 ZL-1 Camaros. This was accomplished at Chevrolet using the Central Office Production Order, or COPO for short. COPO permitted unique and limited production of vehicles with powertrain combinations not available through normal channels. The ZL-1 Camaro had COPO number 9560. The only downside to the deal was the cost of the car: $4,160 on top of the base list price for a V-8 Camaro of $2,727. Gibb had difficulty selling the cars, and persuaded Chevrolet to take back 20 of them for sale to other dealers around the country.

"The ZL-1 Camaros were sold primarily for drag racing in a production environment," Langdon states. "In those cars, we had exhaust manifolds—we didn't have headers—and a full exhaust system which the ZL-1 was never intended to run with. They had to be streetable, but we were trying to do it in an economical way. It was expeditious of us to utilize the production environment to sell these vehicles, knowing most of them were going to run on the drag strip anyway. We did some performance checks to see what the performance penalty was. A ZL-1 with aftermarket headers would produce somewhere in excess of 500 horsepower. We got exactly half that power with exhaust manifolds, exhaust system, mufflers, and pipes as released."

The Tonawanda engine plant states total ZL-1 production was 154 engines. Gibb was the first to take delivery of the ZL-1 Camaro. After being properly set up and checked out by Bill Harrell Performance Center in Missouri, Gibb campaigned the car very successfully. This car became one of the longest distance factory drag cars in history, clocking 30,000 miles—a quarter-mile at a time! Today it is fully restored and still raced, though much less frequently, before countless drag racing fans.

Lesser known are all the other ZL-1 Camaros that were sold and raced. These cars were never thought of as collectable at the time. They were simply race cars. Most succumbed to the harsh environment of the quarter-mile after years of racing.

Only a handful of these cars exist today, lovingly brought back to life when interest in them began to surge in the 1980s.

Drag Racing's Other Stars

Perhaps no driver was more identified with Camaro drag racing in the late 1960s and 1970s than Bill "Grumpy" Jenkins. In 1967, racing against Chrysler 426 Hemis and high-riser Fords, Jenkins won the U.S. National SS/C title at the NHRA Nationals in Indianapolis. Racing a nicely massaged 396, he tripped the lights in 11.55 seconds to take home the trophy and prize money. Ben Wenzel, who won Stock Eliminator with a brand-new B/Stock Z28, joined Jenkins in the U.S. National winner's circle. Dave Strickler drove a Jenkins-prepared Z28 Camaro to the Super Stock World Championship in 1968, defeating Jenkins himself in the final run for the title at the NHRA World Finals in Tulsa, Oklahoma.

The third-generation Camaro became increasingly popular in SCCA events in the 1980s, as improved power, handling- and racing-specific parts became available. The experience gained from this racing resulted in the 1LE package being offered as a production option on the Z28 and IROC-Z in the late 1980s and the 1990s.

The 13th IROC series was held in 1989 and the racing legends continued to pull in enthusiastic fans to watch the battle of the professionals. The driver on the extreme right with his trademark hat needs no introduction. Chevrolet

The IMSA Firehawk racing series was also a hotbed of Camaro racing activity. Mecum Racing's No. 2 and No. 13 spar during the 1989 season. **Chevrolet**

The NHRA instituted a new racing class for 1970 called Pro Stock. Jenkins dominated the early days of Pro Stock with his trademark white 1968 Camaro Rally Sport with big-block V-8 power. In the first Pro Stock event of the 1970 season, Jenkins streaked down the quarter-mile in 9.98 seconds at 138.67 miles per hour, grabbing first place at the Winternationals. Rules changes caused the "bowtie" racers to switch to the small Monza during the mid-1970s, but the Camaro made a comeback on the quarter-mile in the early 1980s. A trio of Texans—David Reher, Buddy Morrison, and Lee Sheperd—dominated Pro Stock racing with their second-generation Z28. They won 6 of 10 NHRA events in 1980. Their driver was Sheperd, who just missed winning the Pro Stock title in 1980, but came back in 1981 to take it home.

The NHRA revised rules again for 1982, upping the Pro Stock displacement limit to 500 cubic inches. Sheperd won six races and the title for that year. Sheperd, in fact, was one of the winningest Pro Stock drivers of the 1980s. Driving for the Reher-Morrison team, he won the NHRA championship in 1983 and 1984, becoming the first driver to win four straight NHRA Pro Stock titles. He also successfully competed in the International Hot Rod Association (IHRA) Pro Stock championships. Sadly, Sheperd's winning career ended when he was killed while testing a race car in 1985. Bruce Allen joined the Reher-Mor-

rison team as principal driver. Allen won eight NHRA and IHRA events in 1985 and set the Pro Stock speed record of 192.71 miles per hour. But drag racing was not the only area where the Camaro had been winning races, pleasing crowds, and building brand loyalty.

The International Race of Champions—IROC

In the mid-1970s a new series was formed that proved to be one of the most successful and popular in America, and an incalculable boon to the Camaro during a time when production performance was all but absent. That series was the International Race of Champions. The premise was to build 12 identical race cars and get the big name professional race car drivers from different motorsports—stock car, drag racing, Trans-Am, and Grand Prix—to race these identical cars in events around the country. With each car professionally and identically prepared as the only common denominator, it was a battle of ability. The series began in 1974 and Porsches were the chosen vehicles. Mark Donohue won the series that year. However, the Porsches were very expensive to set up and maintain for the series, so the backers fished around for something just as fast but more reliable and less expensive to build and operate. Their search ended with the Camaro.

When IROC II, the second season, was scheduled, Roger Penske, along with recently retired Mark Donohue, had the assignment to prepare 15 identical Camaro race cars in only nine weeks. The first development car was driven off a dealership lot in Reading, Pennsylvania. Fourteen more were ordered from the factory with 350-ci small-block V-8s and four-speed manual transmissions; the only difference was the color of their paint.

"The object wasn't to build the world's greatest race car," said Donohue at the time. "It was to build 15 cars with equal potential." Bobby Unser won the first IROC title after the switch to Camaros in 1975, followed by A. J. Foyt's consecutive IROC championships in 1976 and 1977. Tube-framed replicas then replaced the original fleet of production-based IROC Camaros. The tubular space-frame chassis and roll cage was fabricated at stock car specialist Banjo Matthews' shop in North Carolina, and built within the Camaro's second-generation shell. The engine was a 400-plus horsepower race-prepared

350-ci small-block. All other race-hardened components were added to the car at this time.

With these new cars, the level of performance, safety, and reliability improved. Al Unser won the series in 1978, Mario Andretti won in 1979, and Bobby Unser won in 1980. The series was discontinued for several years as new financial backing was arranged and a special IROC facility constructed in Tinton Falls, New Jersey.

The return of the IROC series was announced for 1984, under the direction of its president and general manager, Jay Signore. The third-generation Camaro was the basis for the new cars. Banjo Matthews was again called on to fabricate the tubular chassis, but used only the roof, front and rear glass, door skins and rear bumper facia from the Camaro. The finished chassis was shipped to New Jersey and the IROC technicians went to work. The engine installed was, of course, a 350-ci Chevy small-block. It was a full-race engine built by Katech, Inc., of Mt. Clemens, Michigan. Diversified Plastic of Pontiac, Michigan, designed and manufactured the bulging fiberglass front and rear fenders made to clear the wide Goodyear racing rubber. All the remaining suspension parts, brakes, driveshaft, rear axle, and other components were installed at IROC's facilities. Each car was dynoed to ensure identical output.

The cars were very much like the "stock cars" built to run in NASCAR. Stock car drivers found the new Camaros as comfortable as a pair of old shoes. In the following six years, stock car drivers won the IROC championship four times. They were Cale Yarborough in 1984, Harry Gant in 1985, Geoff Bodine in 1987, and Terry Labonte in 1989. Al Unser, Jr., skilled as an Indy driver, won the title in 1986 and 1988. The series ran for one more year and then was halted. It had been a wild and enjoyable ride for the drivers and a thrill for tens of thousands of race fans.

IMSA/SCCA Showroom Stock

In the mid-1980s still more racing series were launched. The SCCA Showroom Stock and IMSA Street Stock series were efforts to return stock cars to the racetracks. Except for mandatory driver safety equipment, the Camaros that competed in the SCCA Escort Endurance Championship and IMSA Firestone Firehawk Endurance Championship were largely stock. The reliance on factory hardware had given the

Camaro an edge in America's production-based road racing series.

Chevy Camaros racked up 22 wins in the Escort series' GT class from 1985 to 1989, more than three times as many victories as Ford and Porsche. Chevy captured the GT driver's and manufacturer's championships in 1985, 1988, and 1989. Stuart Hayner led a 1-2-3-4 Chevy sweep in the 1988 standings, and the Morrison-Cook Camaro team won 7 of 8 races. In 1989, the Camaro racked up a perfect season, winning 8 out of 8 races. Morrison-Cook teammates Don Knowles and John Heinracy were named co-champions after scoring wins in 8 starts.

The Camaro also topped the list of winning marques in the Firestone Firehawk series with 24 victories in the late 1980s. Camaros won the Grand Sports class manufacturer's championship in 1987, 1989, and 1990. The Camaro was also named the Firehawk Car of the Year in 1989 after earning more points than any other nameplate. In 1989, Chevrolet's John Heinracy won both the SCCA and IMSA titles.

Chevrolet incorporated much of what it had learned from this racing into the G92/1LE option on the Camaro and these pure production cars did extremely well in the 1990s, even while the Camaro made the transition from third generation to fourth generation in 1993. The G4 continued to be the inspiration basis for all forms of drag racing as it raced toward the new millennium. What the future will hold for the Camaro only time will tell, but its brilliant history will always shine.

In 1992 a gathering of racing Camaros celebrated 25 years of Trans-Am racing by Penske and Sharp. Those many years of racing formed the performance parts legacy that made the Camaro one of the most successful production cars to compete on the track. **Chevrolet**

INDEX